INTRODUCTION

The followers of Prince Charles Edward Stuart liked to call themselves the Highland Army, and that is still very largely how they are remembered. Nevertheless, during the months of the Jacobite Rising that army was steadily evolving and changing. The men who stood on Culloden Moor on 16 April 1746 – tired, hungry, and perhaps demoralized though some of them might have been – belonged to what was in some ways a very different, much more professional force than the Highland host which had charged out of the early morning mist at Prestonpans just seven months before.

While the clans always remained the single most important element throughout the army's all too short existence, it was also a surprisingly conventional 18th-century army, with horse, foot, guns, a staff and all the usual supporting elements. Consequently, this study aims to provide a fuller and more rounded picture of what was to all intents and purposes the last Scots army.

At first sight that particular description might seem paradoxical, for of course the Rising of 1745 was not, strictly speaking, a war fought between the Scots and the English. Indeed, there were easily as many Scots fighting for King George as were standing in Prince Charles Edward's ranks; and yet there is no doubt that the Jacobite Army was very much a Scottish army in both character and appearance. Sir Walter Scott perhaps best captured the truth in his novel *Waverley*, written at a time when memories of the rising were still fresh and some of the actors still living. In Sir Walter's eyes, the majority of those who donned the Jacobite white cockade were certainly very consciously fighting for Scotland – but it was for the old Scotland, and for a king at Holyrood again, rather than for the new, outward-looking Scotland that was already at the point of being born when the prince raised his flag: North Britain, standing on the brink of the Enlightenment and the Industrial Revolution.

The irony is that the Stuarts themselves always had their sights very firmly set on London rather than Edinburgh, and initial Jacobite

Prince Charles Edward Stuart wearing Highland dress, by the 19th-century artist Robert Mclan. This is perhaps the most familiar image of the prince, although there appears to be no evidence that he wore the kilt before going on the run after Culloden.

planning was based on the assumption that the uprising would be triggered by a French invasion force landing not in Scotland, but somewhere in the Thames Estuary. French regulars were to do the initial fighting, and the supporters of King James would then be able to rally to his banner under their protection. In this scheme a secondary landing in Scotland was very largely an afterthought; but the abandonment of the proposed French invasion in 1744 changed everything. When they first pledged their support the Highland chiefs had made it absolutely clear that, like their English counterparts, they would only raise their people as auxiliaries to a French army. Yet for the prince there was now no alternative. Embarking but a single company of Franco-Irish volunteers, he sailed for Scotland virtually alone – not because the Highlanders were reckoned to be the oldest and staunchest supporters of the House of Stuart, but because only they could provide him with an army at a moment's notice.

CHRONOLOGY

1745

5 July	Prince Charles Edward clears Belle Isle and sails for Scotland
9 July	Sea fight between *L'Elisabeth* (64) and HMS *Lion* (58)
25 July	Prince lands at Loch nan Uamh in Arisaig
19 August	Standard raised at Glenfinnan
27 August	Rendezvous at Aberchalder – the real beginning of the army
29 August	Unsuccessful attack on Ruthven Barracks
3 Sept	Jacobites 'capture' Perth
18 Sept	Jacobites seize Edinburgh
21 Sept	Jacobite victory at Prestonpans
25 Sept	Jacobites 'capture' Aberdeen
7 Oct	First French blockade runner unloads 2,500 firelocks at Montrose. Three others follow by the end of October, bringing 6 cannon and more small arms
27 Oct	Unsuccessful Jacobite attack on Culloden House, near Inverness
31 Oct	Prince's army marches south from Edinburgh in hopes of triggering an English Jacobite uprising and a French invasion
10–14 Nov	Siege of Carlisle; militia garrison surrenders
20 Nov	Prince's army moves south from Carlisle
24 Nov	First French troops, with 6 heavy guns, land at Montrose
25 Nov	French and Jacobites force HMS *Hazard* to surrender at Montrose
26 Nov	Lord John Drummond and Royal *Écossois* land at Montrose; Irish Picquets land at Peterhead and Aberdeen
29 Nov	Seizure of Manchester
4 Dec	Prince's army enters Derby
6 Dec	With no sign of an English rising or a French invasion, the return to Scotland begins
18 Dec	Rearguard action at Clifton
20 Dec	Prince's army re-crosses border into Scotland
21–30 Dec	Defence of Carlisle; Jacobite garrison surrenders
23 Dec	Jacobite victory at Inverurie, near Aberdeen

1746

4 Jan	Prince's army unites with Lord John Drummond's army
7–8 Jan	Siege of Stirling – burgh surrenders to Jacobites but castle holds out
8–31 Jan	Unsuccessful siege of Stirling Castle
13 Jan	Skirmish at Linlithgow
17 Jan	Jacobite victory at Falkirk
1 Feb	Jacobites withdraw northwards

Elite • 149

The Scottish Jacobite Army 1745–46

Stuart Reid • Illustrated by Gary Zaboly

Consultant editor Martin Windrow

First published in Great Britain in 2006 by Osprey Publishing,
Midland House, West Way, Botley, Oxford OX2 0PH, UK
443 Park Avenue South, New York, NY 10016, USA

Email: info@ospreypublishing.com

© 2006 Osprey Publishing Ltd.

ISBN-10: 1 84603 073 0
ISBN-13: 978 1 84603 073 4

Editor: Martin Windrow
Page layout by Ken Vail Graphic Design, Cambridge, UK
Typeset in Helvetica Neue and ITC New Baskerville
Index by Glyn Sutcliffe
Originated by PPS Grasmere, Leeds, UK
Printed in China through World Print Ltd.

06 07 08 09 10   10 9 8 7 6 5 4 3 2 1

A CIP catalogue record for this book
is available from the British Library

FOR A CATALOGUE OF ALL BOOKS PUBLISHED BY OSPREY MILITARY AND
AVIATION PLEASE CONTACT:

North America:
Osprey Direct, c/o Random House Distribution Center, 400 Hahn Road,
Westminster, MD 21157
Email: info@ospreydirect.com

All other regions:
Osprey Direct UK, PO Box 140, Wellingborough, Northants, NN8 2FA, UK
Email: info@ospreydirect.co.uk

Buy online at **www.ospreypublishing.com**

Artist's Note

Readers may care to note that the original paintings from
which the colour plates in this book were prepared are
available for private sale. All reproduction copyright
whatsoever is retained by the Publishers. All enquiries
should be addressed to:

Gary S.Zaboly,
500 Kappock St, Apt 6F
Riverdale,
Bronx,
NY 10463-6410,
USA

The Publishers regret that they can enter into no
correspondence upon this matter.

11 Feb	Ruthven Barracks surrenders to Glenbuchat
16 Feb	'Rout of Moy' – failed attempt to capture Prince by night raid
18 Feb	Jacobites capture Inverness
21 Feb	Squadron of *Fitzjames Cavallerie* lands at Aberdeen
25 Feb	Picquet of *Régiment Berwick* lands at Peterhead
3–5 Mar	Siege of Fort Augustus; garrison from Guise's Regt surrenders
10 Mar	'Atholl Raid'
10–31 Mar	Unsuccessful siege of Blair Castle
20 Mar	Jacobite victory at Dornoch; skirmish at Keith
20 Mar–2 Apr	Unsuccessful Jacobite siege of Fort William
26 Mar	Second picquet of *Berwick* captured at Tongue, with £12,000 in gold
12 April	British army crosses River Spey; rearguard action at Nairn
15 April	Cromartie's brigade ambushed and destroyed at Embo; unsuccessful Jacobite attempt to surprise British camp at Nairn
16 April	Battle of Culloden
18 April	Jacobite Army disperses at Fort Augustus and Ruthven Barracks
19 April	Last French units surrender
2 May	Sea fight in Loch nan Uamh
27 May	Last Jacobite regiments disband

RAISING THE ARMY

Prince Charles Edward was not disappointed in his expectations of quickly finding himself at the head of an army; although a number of the chiefs on whom he was counting determinedly stayed at home, the support of those who did turn out – headed by Cameron of Locheil – was crucial, since each of them brought at least the semblance of a regiment. These first clan levies, raised far more quickly than would have been possible anywhere else in Scotland or England, formed the little army that defeated General Cope at Prestonpans on 21 September. In truth, at that stage it was hardly worthy of the name of an army, amounting to barely 2,500 men; but after that first vital victory it formed the nucleus around which a much larger force was formed.

At Edinburgh, during the five weeks following the battle, it doubled in size, as the clans were joined by other units raised from nearly all over Scotland, excepting the old Covenanting south-west. Although these new regiments, and a number of others that remained in Scotland to form the nucleus of a second army gathering at Perth, were frequently referred to as the Low Country Foot, this was very much an oversimplification. The Duke of Perth's Regiment – the only 'Lowland' unit to fight at Prestonpans – had both Highland and Lowland companies, and in fact a substantial proportion of the men in many of these supposed Lowland regiments were actually of Highland extraction. This was certainly true of those men raised in the upland areas of Aberdeenshire and

A more conventional 18th-century image of a younger but quite recognizable Prince Charles Edward, in the conventional half-armour favoured for aristocratic portraits. On a number of occasions he was described as wearing 'French' clothes such as these.

Highland Visitors – a contemporary propaganda piece by J.Dubois, purporting to show Jacobites plundering an English village. The figures look surprisingly convincing – note the officer in trews at centre.

Banffshire – in Strathbogie, Strathavan and Speyside by John Gordon of Avochie and old John Gordon of Glenbuchat. Even the three regiments of the Athole Brigade, from central Perthshire, were officially accounted part of the Lowland division. There was, perhaps with good reason, a decided feeling that the Highlanders serving in these particular regiments were a good deal less 'wild' than the ones from the west. While this might arguably have been the case, the real difference was that they were raised by the personal exertions of their officers rather than called or forced out as clan levies.

Clansmen and feudal levies

In theory, the raising of a clan regiment was simple enough: as one of Robert Louis Stevenson's characters wryly declared, 'when the piper plays the clan must dance'. The chief first called upon his 'people', that is his tacksmen (those who leased land from him), 'near relations, friends and partakers' to come out and, if they were in agreement, each in turn brought out their own tenants, servants and followers. It was thus possible quite literally to raise a regiment overnight – although arming it properly, and keeping the men in the ranks in the long term, sometimes proved a good deal more difficult. Even at the very beginning, not all of the men came out readily. A fairly typical government intelligence report recounted that 'upon Thursday the 15th August Cameron of Kinlochlyon [sic], Cameron of Blairchierr, Cameron of Blairmachult, Cameron of Glenevis, and Cameron alias MacKalonie of Strone, heads of the several tribes of the name of

Cameron, came from Locheil's country and entered Rannoch with a party of servants and followers to the number of about 24 and went from house to house on both sides of Loch Rannoch... and intimate to all the Camerons, which are pretty numerous on both sides of the loch, that, if they did not forthwith go with them, that they would that instant proceed to burn all their houses and hough their cattle; whereupon they carried off the Rannoch men, about one hundred, mostly of the name of Cameron...'

No fewer than 57 out of 87 men from Glen Urquhart and Glenmoriston who surrendered in May 1746 were variously noted to have been 'forced', 'pressed', or in one case 'dragd out'. Similarly, the Rev William Gordon of Alvie declared that out of 43 of his parishioners caught up in the rising, only three had gone voluntarily – the rest were forced out by 'burning their houses, carrying off their cattle, and breaking their heads'. Nor was this all; there was an express sent from Alex MacDonald of Keppoch, the 15th, intimating to Alex Macdonald in Drumchastle and Alexander MacDonald of Dalchosney, the informer's father, both in the Duke of Athole's lands of Bunrannoch, that if they did not immediately go and join him, Keppoch, they would be proceeded against with burning and houghing as above...'[1]

Highlander wearing the philabeg or 'little kilt', from MacIan's *Clans of the Scottish Highlands.* Working in the Victorian period, MacIan researched his subject thoroughly, and although the clan tartans (in this case Grant) are not contemporary, the clothing styles are accurate. Note the early box-pleating of the kilt, the sleeve vent of the short jacket, and the light shoes held on by laces around the instep and ankle.

Keppoch was evidently a firm believer in employing coercion. The minister of Lochbroom afterwards testified that on 17 March 1746, Keppoch and some of his men turned up there and 'unexpectedly surprised the poor people, snatching some of them out of their beds. Others, who thought their old age would excuse them, were dragged from their ploughs... while some were taken off the highways. One I did myself see overtaken by speed of foot and when he declared he would rather die than be carried to the rebellion, was knock'd to the ground by the butt of a musket and carried away all bleed.'

What is significant about this particular incident is that the Lochbroom men were not actually Keppoch's clansmen at all, and most of those press-ganged by him on this occasion went into the Earl of Cromartie's Regiment. Allied to the clan system was the even more widespread and equally archaic concept of vassalage – an ancient obligation on a man to turn out in arms at the behest of his landlord or feudal superior. The Athole Brigade was largely recruited in this fashion; and in a typical exchange early in the rising, the Jacobite Duke William wrote to his 'vassals' in the Dunkeld area that 'As... you and the

It would probably be difficult to find a better illustration of why men in Scotland were generally referred to by the name of their dwelling or estate, rather than simply by their surnames.

Another grim-looking left-handed swordsman by the Penicuik artist, this time identified as Alexander MacDonald of Keppoch. Merciless during the levying of the prince's army, Keppoch would be killed at the head of his regiment at Culloden. (Author's copy)

rest of my Vassalls & tenants do not bestir yourselves with that activity that becomes Loyal Subjects… I once more require you peremtorely… to raise in arms all the men you can, and meet in Pitlochrie.'

Despite this stern summons, a few days later John Stewart of Stenton responded that 'the whole inhabitants there are quite degenerate from their ancestors, and not one spark of loyalty among them; no one of them will stir without force'. Nor did matters improve thereafter; in January 1746 Duke William was still complaining of the 'unspeakable difficulty' he was experiencing in persuading men to rise. Even when they did come out, the desertion rate in the Athole Brigade is reckoned to have been the worst of any Jacobite unit.[2]

This form of recruiting was not by any means confined to the Athole Brigade, but extended to a number of other areas where local families exercised a traditional influence over their neighbours and tenants. In the north-east, for example, the formidable Lady Erroll certainly forced out a number of her tenants to join the regiment of Footguards being raised by her son-in-law, Lord Kilmarnock. The Earl of Cromartie's Regiment – as described above – was a similar case; and Alexander McGrowther claimed that as a landholder under the Duke of Perth 'it was the custom to obey commands', while Peter Maclaren similarly spoke of a 'general notion that they must obey' him as their landlord.

Obviously enough, the quality of many of these sometimes reluctant recruits left a lot to be desired. Captain John MacLean rather blandly recounted how on his march to join the Prince's army, 'we catched a Deserter in a moor in Our Way but after two or three miles travelling with us we let him Goe he being 70 years old only [we] took his Sword for one of our men'.

Nevertheless, it would be a mistake to assume that all of the men standing in the ranks were pulled unwillingly on to the heather by the arbitrary power of their chiefs or their feudal superiors – or indeed, that obedience to their chiefs was the sole determining factor in bringing them out.

Volunteers

Other than the clan and feudal levies, the officers and men following the Prince fell into several different categories. First and most important were the volunteers, who freely joined the Jacobite Army, if for a surprising variety of reasons.

One contemporary remarked that at first 'the Rebellion was favoured by almost all the common people. The promise of freeing them from the Malt Tax had a surprising influence upon them, this being a tax the

---

2 Confusingly, there were two Dukes of Athole above ground at the same time. Duke William was an attainted Jacobite who returned from exile with Prince Charles Edward, and is better known as the Marquis of Tullibardine. His younger brother, Duke John, was a supporter of the government, but prudently took himself off to Bath until all was over. Both were elder brothers of Lord George Murray.

Farmers are especially sensible of... The Rebels therefore hitherto behaving civilly, listing only volunteers, paying freely, taking but some few good horses and arms as they met them, and freeing the country people from the eternal dread they were under of the Malt Gaugers, were looked upon by them as the deliverers of their country.'

While the single most important reason for volunteering undoubtedly seems to have been a widespread desire to re-establish Scotland's independence, other factors ranged from genuine enthusiasm for the Jacobite cause (or at least a strong objection to the present government, which was not quite the same thing), all the way to simple peer pressure or even a sense of adventure. Even so the decision was rarely taken lightly; for instance, the Glen Urquhart men only committed themselves to the rising after a lengthy and mature debate held one Sunday in Kilmore churchyard.

Then again, while some joined the rebel ranks from conviction, hope or curiosity, more than a few were suspected of running away from debts and the prospect of bankruptcy. Of James Moir of Stonywood it was said that, 'This gentleman very early imbibed the Jacobite principles and was entirely educated that way; his fortune also was greatly embarrassed, so that his going off was no great surprise.' Similarly, the reason for John Hamilton of Sandstoun's involvement 'was generally imagined to be owing to the disorder of his affairs'. It was remarked that while several merchants of note had joined in the previous rising of 1715, this time around there were 'none but a few smugglers, and a very few tradesmen'.

Whatever their motivation, while some of the volunteers accepted commissions and set about recruiting men of their own, many came in singly or in groups, with perhaps just a handful of friends and followers. Thus, two of Grant of Shewglie's sons set off one morning with 'a dozen young fellows'. Others again were recruited in more conventional fashion; John Crawford of the Duke of Perth's Regiment was seen 'with a White Cockade and sergeants halberd, along with a drummer, beating up for recruits for the rebels in Edinburgh', exactly as his regular counterparts might have done. Few, however, can have been treated to speeches such as the one delivered by Jemmy Dawson at Derby:

"All gentlemen volunteers who are willing to serve His Royal Highness Charles, Prince of Wales, Regent of Scotland and Ireland, in one of His Royal Highnesses new raised English regiments, commonly called the Manchester Regiment, under the command of Colonel Townley, let them repair to the Drum Head or to the Colonel's headquarters where they shall be kindly entertained, enter into present pay and good quarters, receive all arms and accoutrements and everything fit to complete a gentleman soldier, and for their further encouragement, when

This member of the Black Watch depicted in the 1742 *Cloathing Book* also provides a pretty good image of a typical soldier in the Jacobite Army three years later. Note the use of a belly-box in place of the more usual large cartridge box worn on the right hip, which would be hampered by the belted plaid. The plaid was put on first, directly over the shirt, and arranged into a kilt below the waist; it was then belted, and the upper part hung in folds from the waist. After the waistcoat and jacket had been donned, the end of the plaid was carried up outside them behind the shoulder, and pinned.

9

Simon Fraser the elder, Lord Lovat (1667–1747). Although too old to play an active military role, Lovat raised two battalions from amongst his clansmen, and – according to witnesses at his trial – provided them with tents marked with his crest, and camp colours, one of which was found at Culloden. His age did not save this incorrigible intriguer from execution.

they arrive in London they shall receive 5 guineas each and a crown to drink his Majesty King James health, and, if not willing to serve any longer, they shall have a full discharge. Every man shall be rewarded according to his merits. God Bless King James!"

He got few if any takers; and once the first flush of enthusiasm had passed, willing recruits generally became progressively harder to find and retain. In the end not only did the 'forcing' of men into the clan regiments become ever more brutal, but even in Lowland areas the Jacobites resorted to levying men under something akin to the old Scots fencible system.

Conscripts and mercenaries

Utilizing the existing tax records, the Jacobites demanded that landowners should supply one able-bodied and properly clothed and equipped man for every £100 (Scots) of valued rent. Unsurprisingly, this proved decidedly unpopular. Lord Lewis Gordon commented in December 1745 that 'Although I have got some volunteers, I assure you that att least two thirds of the men I have raised is by the stipulation att first agreed on, and all those that have not as yet sent in their quotas, have been wrote to in very strong terms.'

The tenor of those threats can be imagined from instructions issued to some of Gordon's officers, who were to 'require from the heritors, factors, or tenants, as you shall think most proper, an able-bodied man for his Majesty King James's service, with sufficient Highland cloaths, plaid and arms, for each 100£ of their valued rent, or the sum of 5£ sterl. Money for each of the above men, to be paid to J.M. of Stonywood, or his order of Aberdeen: and in case of refusal of the men or money, you are forthwith to burn all the houses, corn and planting upon the foresaid estates.' These threats were effective: 'the burning of a single house or farm stack in a Parish terrified the whole, so that they would quickly send in their proportion, and by this means, with the few that joined as volunteers, he [Lord Lewis Gordon] raised near 300 men called the Strathboggy Battalion in the country thereabouts.'

How those quotas were actually filled is one of the more intriguing aspects of the affair. When an accounting came to be made afterwards, the lists compiled for the government of those involved in the rising were careful to distinguish between those men who were volunteers, those who were or may have been 'forced' (generally by far the greater number), and those who were 'hired out by the County' or as paid substitutes by individuals.

In Banffshire alone, where a substantial part of the Strathbogie Regiment was recruited, no fewer than one-third of those reported to have been with the rebels were recorded as having been 'hired out by the county'. In Forfarshire it seems to have been more common for individuals to hire substitutes to serve in Lord Ogilvy's Regiment. Charles Mather, a ploughman from Montrose, was 'hired by a farmer in his stead', as were James Miller from Glamis and Alexander Robertson from Forfar, while other men, such as David Scott, also from Forfar, were 'hired by the county.' Since they had clearly enlisted for money alone, these hired men were rarely treated as real rebels, or at least were not considered to be quite as culpable as those who joined the rising from ideological or other motives. Consequently, a disproportionate number of them were left undisturbed afterwards or, if they had been captured, were statistically far more likely to be turned loose (or drafted into the ranks of the British Army) rather than transported or brought to trial; clearly, it was not thought worthwhile to prosecute them even by way of example.

RIGHT **Not all of the Penicuik artist's subjects were Jacobites, and these sketches depict Loyalist volunteers from the Edinburgh area at drill. They are dressed largely as would be their Jacobite counterparts in John Roy Stuart's Regiment. The central man, wearing a bonnet, is specifically identified as coming from Penicuik. One of the right-hand figures wears a long caped riding coat, slit for access to his sword hilt – see also Plate B1. (Author's copies)**

BELOW **A fine study by Maclan of a Highland gentleman wearing the belted plaid. Note how the bonnet is adjusted by tapes at the back.**

Turncoats

However, the government was a good deal less lenient when it came to another group: former members of the British Army. It is common for all of these men to be referred to as deserters, but in reality very few men deliberately absented themselves from their units in order to join the Jacobites, and most of those who did were drawn there by close family ties. Instead, the majority of British Army personnel found serving in the rebel ranks were actually former prisoners of war. In the first place there were men belonging to the Highland Independent Companies or to Loudoun's newly raised 64th Highlanders. Although technically British soldiers, few of them had ever had the chance to actually wear King George's red coat before their capture, and changing sides had required little persuasion, especially if their officers led the way. Cluny MacPherson was only the most prominent of them, exchanging a captaincy in the 64th for command of his own clan regiment. Consequently, those men subsequently recaptured were as a rule treated as rebels rather than turned over to the Army for punishment. It is a measure of their lack of commitment that there are a number of instances of men cheerfully defecting back again to King George's service in one or other of the Independent Companies.

The enlistment of prisoners captured at Prestonpans was altogether a different matter. Just how many of Sir John Cope's men changed sides after their capture is hard to assess, but largely anecdotal evidence points to a fairly sizeable number. A witness named Robert Bowey reported that 'On Friday last 27th Sept he was at Edinburgh and there saw about 200 soldiers with the livery of HM King George go down under guard to the Abby, and shortly after saw about 40 carried away under guard... and the remainder set at liberty, and this deponent saw many going about at large with white cockades along with the rebels, by reason whereof it was said that they had all initiated the Pretender and were in his service.'

Judging by references in Jacobite orderly books to 'the redcoats of Perth's and John Roy Stuart's', most if not all of them seem to have ended up in those regiments; the adjutant of Perth's Regiment, John Christie, was formerly a sergeant in one of Cope's regiments.

In the third category were men who enlisted into regiments of the French Army's Irish Brigade. Some of them were indeed genuine deserters, who had crossed the lines in Flanders months before coming to Scotland with the Irish Picquets or the *Royal Écossois*. However, the single largest concentration were members of Guise's 6th Foot, captured at either Inverness or Fort Augustus and then press-ganged into the French service. In his accounting of the French forces at Culloden the French 'ambassador' to the rebel forces, the Marquis d'Eguilles, recorded the remarkable figure of 148 prisoners and deserters out of a total of 260 serving in the Irish Piquets – a full 60 per cent. After Culloden, where 81 of them were captured, their prospects must have seemed bleak. As many as 28 of them may have been hanged almost immediately; but the rest were in fact released and returned to their units after the intercession of a local minister named Alexander McBean, who was able to confirm just how badly the men of Guise's had been treated in captivity.

William Boyd, Earl of Kilmarnock (1704–1746). Initially Kilmarnock raised and led a troop of cavalry in the Falkirk/Stirling area, which were designated as Horse Grenadiers. In early 1746 it was dismounted and its horses turned over to Fitzjames's Horse, so Kilmarnock raised a new regiment which was designated as the Footguards. Captured at Culloden, he was executed on 18 August 1746.

ORGANIZATION

Whatever their origin or circumstances, all of these men – Highlanders, Lowlanders, volunteers, levies or mercenaries – belonged to regiments which were at least outwardly organized on conventional lines, although the terminology involved can sometimes be misleading. In the British Army of the day the terms 'regiment' and 'battalion' were interchangeable, since nearly all of its infantry regiments consisted of a single battalion. The same was true of most Jacobite regiments, which tended to average 200–300 men, and rarely exceeded 500; some fielded two or more battalions, but there was little consistency in the practice.

The first to do so was the Duke of Athole's Regiment, which fielded two battalions at Prestonpans, and three single-battalion regiments thereafter as the Athole Brigade. For the march into England a second, rather *ad hoc* battalion raised in Aberdeenshire was added to the Duke of Perth's Regiment; this was a temporary expedient, however, and on the regiment's return to Scotland the second

EARL of KILMARNOCK

battalion was broken up and the survivors transferred to Lord Lewis Gordon's Regiment. Like the Athole Brigade, the latter eventually comprised at least three battalions, raised in Aberdeenshire and Banffshire by John Gordon of Avochie, James Moir of Stonywood and Francis Farquharson of Monaltrie; in fact Lord Lewis never actually took the field at their head, and to all intents and purposes they operated as independent units.

Another regiment, Lord Ogilvy's, was originally a single-battalion unit from Forfarshire, but was joined on its return to Scotland by a second battalion raised there in the meantime by Sir James Kinloch. It was a similar story with two of the clan regiments. MacDonnell of Glengarry's Regiment at first had a single battalion which went right through the campaign from beginning to end, but a second one led by Coll MacDonald of Barisdale fought at Falkirk, only to miss Culloden through having been sent north in a vain attempt to recover some lost French gold. The other regiment, Lovat's, had one battalion at Falkirk and would have been joined by a second on the field at Culloden if the battle had not been lost before they arrived. To add to the confusion, it was also fairly common for reinforcements to be brought together as a battalion which operated independently only until it caught up with its parent regiment, and was then absorbed into it.

Many so-called regiments were wretchedly small and over-officered. The Adjutant General, Colonel Sullivan, wryly commented that at the outset of the rising: 'All was confused… They must go by tribes; such a chiefe of a tribe had sixty men, another thirty, another twenty, more or lesse; they would not mix nor separate, & wou'd have double officers, yt is two Captns & two Lts, to each Compagny, strong or weak. That was uselesse… but by little and little, they were brought into a certain regulation'.

That there were too many officers is indisputable, and the problem was by no means confined to the Highland regiments – it was particularly acute in the cavalry. 'There were several little people in Banffshire and Buchan, etc.,' commented one observer, 'who raised a few men each, and joined the Lord Lieutenant [Lord Lewis Gordon] and all got commissions of one kind or another, which was by no means hard to be obtained.' Generally speaking, these commissions were granted not as a reward for bringing in those few men, but in the hope that the officers granted them might find some more.

In the meantime, the smaller units were normally attached to larger ones; for example both the MacKinnons and the Glencoe men were immediately joined to Keppoch's MacDonalds while both the Glen Urquhart and Glenmoriston men were attached to Glengarry's Regiment. The MacLachlans were for some reason at first attached not to another clan regiment but to Lord Nairne's Regiment in the Athole Brigade, before eventually being formed into a composite regiment with the Macleans shortly before Culloden.

Arthur Elphinstone, Lord Balmerino (1688–1746). As the Hon Arthur Elphinstone, he raised the smaller of the two troops of Lifeguards; surrendering after Culloden, he was executed with Lord Kilmarnock on 18 August 1746. Accounts of his death note that he wore his troop's uniform of a blue coat turned up with red.

The consolidation process was a flexible one, and if required some of these smaller units could just as readily be detached again for a specific purpose. As a rule 18th-century commanders were reluctant to weaken their forces by sending complete regiments on detached service – particularly if there was a danger of their being cut off – and preferred instead to use consolidated formations made up of several small detachments. Therefore, when a column was assembled to recover the consignment of gold seized from a French blockade runner forced ashore in Sutherland, only one major unit – the Earl of Cromartie's Regiment – was assigned to the expedition, and that only because it was raised locally to the search area. The balance of the force was made up of minor units such as Barisdale's battalion, MacGregor of Glengyle's men and the Mackinnons. (In military terms this was eminently sensible, but had this particular collection of banditti ever caught up with the gold, one is bound to wonder how much of it would have found its way to Inverness thereafter.)

Just as in other armies, each Jacobite regiment was in turn made up of a number of companies of anything up to 50 or 60 men, though usually much fewer. Exactly how many companies there actually were varied from unit to unit, but five or six companies seem to have been quite common, rather than the ten normally constituting a regular battalion. Interestingly, at least three regiments – Glengarry's, Locheil's and Lord Ogilvy's – are known to have had grenadier companies, so perhaps others did too, although there seems to be no surviving evidence as to how their personnel might have been distinguished.

Highland officer and sergeant in British Crown service, taken from Francis Grose's *Military Antiquities* and in turn copied from prints by Van Gucht dating to the 1740s. Although these are regular soldiers, either of the 43rd/42nd Black Watch or Loudon's 64th Highlanders, their Jacobite counterparts can have looked little different.

INFANTRY UNITS

Athole Brigade Although mainly raised in Highland Perthshire in the early weeks of the rising, this large regiment was not a clan but a feudal levy, and served throughout the campaign as part of the Lowland division. Some aspects of its organization are unclear. It was originally known as the Duke of Athole's Regiment, but at Edinburgh the two battalions that fought at Prestonpans were joined by a third, and shortly thereafter these were re-designated as regiments within what was termed the Athole Brigade. The changes in title are first noted in orderly books on 19 November 1745, but they may well have been in informal use for some time before that date. The two original battalions/regiments were

BELOW Besides the Cameron banner (see bottom page 17), at least 14 other colours and flags were captured at Culloden, and descriptions survive on a receipt given for them by Major Hu Wentworth of the 6th Foot on 11 May 1746:

'(1) On a staff a white linen colours belonging to the Farquharsons
(2) On a staff a white linen colours, motto *Terrores Furio*, Chisholmes
(3) On a staff a large plain white colours, said to be the standard
(4) On a staff a blue silk colours, *Sursum Tendo*
(5) A staff the colours tore off
(6) Do.
(7) On a staff a white silk colours with the Stewarts Arms *God Save King*
(8) On a staff a white silk colours, in the canton St.Andrews cross
(9) On a staff a white silk with a red saltire
(10) A blew silk colours with the Lovat arms *Sine Sanguine Victor*
(11) A white silk with a blue saltire
(12) Piece of blue silk with a St.Andrew saltire *Commit the Work to God*
(13) A white linen jaik with a red saltire
(14) One of Lord Lovat's camp colours'
Illustrated here are numbers 9 and 11 on Wentworth's list.

Lord Nairne's and Lord George Murray's (the latter actually being commanded by Robert Mercer of Aldie), and the third was Archibald Menzies of Shian's. There is some suggestion that a fourth battalion may have existed for a time, but this was most likely a reinforcement draft rather than a discrete formation. For most of the campaign the brigade also included a small unit commanded by the Laird of MacLachlan which was generally attached to Lord Nairne's Regiment. Theoretically the brigade still 'belonged' to the Duke of Athole, but it was generally regarded as Lord George Murray's, although he in turn delegated day-to-day command to Nairne. The brigade suffered badly from desertion, and none of its regiments seems to have consistently mustered many more than 200 men. After Culloden, where it was seriously engaged for the first time and suffered heavy losses, the survivors probably dispersed at Fort Augustus on or about 18 April 1746.

Bannerman of Elsick's Regiment A very small regiment of no more than 150 men, raised by Sir Alexander Bannerman of Elsick in the Stonehaven area (just south of Aberdeen) after Prestonpans, and largely employed on internal security duties. Finlayson's map of Culloden shows the regiment standing in the left rear of the army near King's Stables, but it is more likely that it was absorbed into Lord Kilmarnock's Footguards some time in March 1746. A white colour with a St Andrew saltire in the canton is illustrated, and may have been carried by the regiment.

Cameron of Locheil's Regiment Effectively the first to be raised, this was always one of the strongest Jacobite units and was generally regarded as an elite, although initially very badly armed. Donald Cameron of Locheil brought some 750 men to the gathering at Glenfinnan on 19 August, but 150 of them were subsequently sent home because they were unarmed, and straggling reduced the regiment to about 500 at Prestonpans. While the army was in England, Ludovic Cameron of Torcastle levied out a further 300 men for the regiment, so it still appears to have been about 700 strong at Culloden. Although suffering heavy losses there it was not disbanded until 27 May 1746. Two colours are known and illustrated, one being a simple red- and yellow-striped banner, and the other a red banner bearing the arms of Cameron of Glendessary.

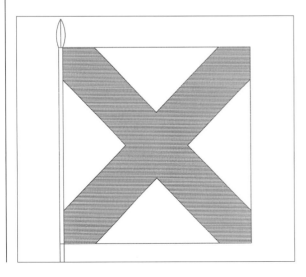

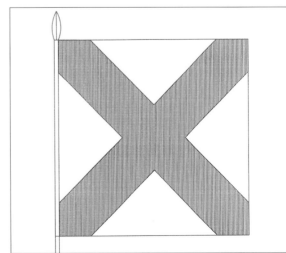

Chisholms of Strathglass This very small unit, effectively an independent company no more than about 80 strong, was led by Roderick Og Chisholm. Surprisingly, it did not join the army until March 1746, and then reputedly suffered very heavy casualties at Culloden, where it was effectively destroyed. A white colour with the Chisholm motto was taken from the unit, and is illustrated.

Crichton of Auchingoul's Regiment (see Plate C2). This very small unit was raised in and around Aberdeen and Old Meldrum late in 1745 by James Crichton of Auchingoul. There is some uncertainty over his rank: he appears to have held a colonel's commission, but at one stage he was referred to as a captain in the Duke of Perth's Regiment – although this may only have been a device to prevent his few men from being taken over by Lord Lewis Gordon. The last reference in orderly books to 'Crichton's regiment' as an independent unit occurs on 10 March 1746, and very shortly afterwards they were apparently absorbed into Kilmarnock's Footguards. William Mackenzie afterwards confessed that 'he did bear Arms in a Company of Kilmarnock's Rebel Regiment, commanded by James CRICHTON of Auchingowl, Captain.'

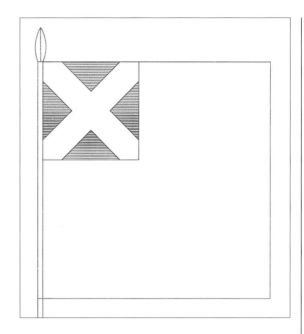

ABOVE **No.8 on Wentworth's list was this unidentified colour. The same flag does appear on the arms of Bannerman of Elsick, however – an allusion to the family's hereditary office – and so it may belong to the little regiment raised by Sir Alexander Bannerman.**

LEFT **These red-and-gold barred colours appear to have been captured from the Camerons at Culloden but were not included in the official list of trophies. Their present whereabouts are unknown, but in the 19th century they were still preserved in a frame and (wrongly) identified as belonging to the Prince's Lifeguards.**

Still preserved at Achnacarry, these colours were also said to have been carried by the Camerons. In the centre of the red field is a green panel bearing a variant of the Cameron arms, differing from those of Locheil by the arm and sword crest in place of his own bundle of arrows. This is probably the 'ruddy banner' of the Camerons of Glendessary, which James Philip of Almericlose saw at Dalcomera in 1689.

BELOW **Second on Wentworth's list was 'a white linen colours, motto** *Terrores Furio*, **Chisholmes'. The motto was actually** *Feros Ferio*, **which suggests a transcription error by a harassed clerk. The Chisholm arms bear two mottos, but this one forms part of the crest, as reconstructed here.**

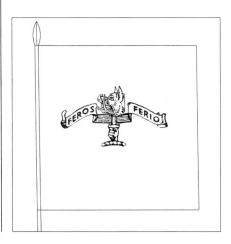

Earl of Cromartie's Regiment Although raised in the northern highlands after Prestonpans by George Mackenzie, Earl of Cromartie and his son, John Mackenzie, Lord Macleod, and very substantially made up of Mackenzies, this was not really a clan levy. Some of the men turned out as tenants and followers of Cromartie, but otherwise it was the usual mixture of volunteers and pressed men. 'Highland clothes' were being made up for the regiment in October 1745. It was approximately 200 strong at Falkirk, but having been sent north in search of the French gold it was then ambushed and destroyed in a running fight with Loyalist militia at Embo near Golspie on 15 April 1746. It is possible that a blue colour bearing a white saltire and the Sinclair motto was carried by one of the regiment's companies.

Farquharson of Monaltrie's Battalion (see Plate B1). This was sometimes referred to as the 'Mar' battalion of Lord Lewis Gordon's Regiment, having been raised in Braemar and upper Deeside by Francis Farquharson of Monaltrie. Most (but evidently not all) of the men in the ranks were Highlanders, and they even included a party of MacGregors under the laird of Inverenzie. When James Logie saw them in Aberdeen they 'were dressed in highland clothes mostly', so presumably a significant number must have been in Lowland dress. Both Monaltrie himself and a plain white colour belonging to the regiment were taken at Culloden, where the unit had fought in the first line.

John Gordon of Avochie's Battalion (see Plate B2 and B3). Sometimes referred to as the 'Strathbogie' Battalion of Lord Lewis Gordon's Regiment. Many of the 300 or so men in the ranks were Highlanders, but for the most part it was comprised of feudal levies and mercenaries rather than clansmen. An intelligence report of 11 December 1745 declared that of the 300 men, 'only 100 have joined [volunteered?]; mostly herds and hiremen from about Strathbogie and unacquainted with the use of arms; many are pressed and intend to desert…'. After serving at Inverurie, Falkirk and Culloden it was disbanded at Ruthven Barracks on 18 April 1746. References to plain white colours like those carried by Monaltrie's Mar battalion can be linked to this unit.

John Gordon of Glenbuchat's Regiment '…[He] soon got together about 300 men mostly from Strathdawn and Glenlivit and some too from Strathboggy, all parts of the Duke of Gordon's Estate. His son-in-law, Mr Forbes of Skeleter [Lieutenant Colonel George Forbes of Skellater], also brought him some of his corps from Strathdon, a country belonging mostly to gentlemen of that name, formerly vassals of the Earl of Mar, now of the Lord Braco.' Although taking part in the march to Derby the regiment was not present at Falkirk, being assigned instead to blockade Stirling Castle, but it was at Culloden and afterwards probably disbanded at Ruthven Barracks on 18 April 1746. On its arrival at Edinburgh it was equipped with arms taken from Cope's army. A white colour bearing the ducal arms survives and is illustrated.

Lord Lewis Gordon's Regiment This large regiment was raised in Aberdeenshire and Banffshire after Prestonpans by Lord Lewis Gordon, a renegade naval officer and son of the Duke of Gordon. The constituent battalions are listed here separately under their commanding officers: **Francis Farquharson of Monaltrie, John Gordon of Avochie** and **James Moir of Stonywood**. A number of references suggest that all battalions had plain white colours.

Grant of Glenmoriston's Battalion (see Plate A1). A small unit from Glenmoriston and Glen Urquhart, averaging about 80–100 men led by Major Patrick Grant of Glenmoriston and Captain (?) Alexander Grant, younger of Shewglie. Raised in September 1745, it arrived in Edinburgh on 20 September, just in time to take part in the battle of Prestonpans, where it was attached to McDonnell of Glengarry's Regiment. Subsequently it went with Glengarry's into England, and then north for a time with Barisdale after Falkirk. It was then levied out again in strength by Shewglie, and rejoined the army on the afternoon of 15 April 1746. Some 30 men were killed at Culloden; both Glenmoriston and Shewglie escaped, but 87 of their men who survived the campaign surrendered on 4 May, and nearly all were transported.

Lord Kilmarnock's Footguards This was a composite regiment formed in March 1746 by combining the then-dismounted Lord Kilmarnock's Horse and Lord Pitsligo's Horse with James Crichton of Auchingoul's

Regiment, and adding some new recruits from Aberdeenshire forced out by Kilmarnock's formidable mother-in-law, Lady Erroll. Bannerman of Elsick's little regiment was probably consolidated with it as well, and consequently both Johnstone and Elcho state that the Footguards were over 200 strong at Culloden. A magnificent colour bearing 'the Stewarts arms' almost certainly belonged to this regiment, and is illustrated.

Lord Lovat's Regiment '…[The] whole posse of Frasers was formed into three regiments… commanded by the Master of Lovat, Charles Fraser of Inverallochie and James Fraser of Foyers.' The latter certainly commanded the force that unsuccessfully attacked Culloden House on 27 October 1745, but it was afterwards taken over by the elderly Lord Lovat's son, the Master of Lovat. About 300 men fought at Falkirk, and Inverallochie's battalion had about the same at Culloden, but the Master of Lovat's battalion missed taking part in the battle by a matter of hours and probably disbanded later that day. A blue colour 'with the Lovat arms' was captured at Culloden, and is illustrated.

MacDonnell of Barisdale's Regiment Coll MacDonnell of Barisdale was one of those who joined the Jacobites at Aberchalder on 27 August 1745, where he and his men were attached to Glengarry's Regiment. After Prestonpans he returned home to raise more men, and did not rejoin the army until shortly before the battle of Falkirk, where his regiment

ABOVE **No.7 on Wentworth's list was this 'white silk colours with the Stewarts Arms *God Save King*'. As reconstructed here the arms are those of Prince Charles Edward as they appear on the colours of his short-lived French *Régiment d'Albany*. The resemblance to those carried by the Scots Guards – other than the white field – may not be coincidental, since they were probably carried by Lord Kilmarnock's Footguards.**

RIGHT **No.10 on Wentworth's list was a 'blew silk colours with the Lovat arms *Sine Sanguine Victor*'. This reconstruction copies the description literally, although the motto is not Lovat's – it is just possible that the arms displayed were actually those of Charles Fraser of Inverallochy, the Aberdeenshire laird who led one of Lovat's battalions at Culloden. If so, the arms would not have been quartered, and would have featured a crescent between the three cinquefoils representing *fraises* or strawberry flowers. Although No.14, 'One of Lord Lovat's camp colours', is not otherwise described on Wentworth's list, a witness at Lovat's trial testified that both camp colours and tents bore Lovat's crest (the stag's head shown here).**

effectively served as the second battalion of Glengarry's. Having been sent north in a vain attempt to recover the gold landed from *Le Prince Charles*, it missed the battle of Culloden and was disbanded on or about 26 May 1746.

MacDonald of Clanranald's Regiment Three companies were present when the standard was raised at Glenfinnan on 19 August 1745, and about 200 men fought at Prestonpans under Ranald MacDonald, younger of Clanranald. Reinforcements are said to have brought it up to some 350 strong at Falkirk, but only 200 were present at Culloden, where Clanranald was wounded. The regiment was disbanded at Fort Augustus on or about 18 April 1746.

MacDonald of Glencoe's Regiment A very small unit numbering no more than 120 men commanded by Alexander MacDonald of Glencoe. Joining the Jacobites at Aberchalder on 27 August 1745, it served throughout the campaign attached to MacDonald of Keppoch's Regiment, and surrendered to General Campbell on 12 May 1746, having lost 52 killed and 36 wounded. Instead of a conventional stand of colours they are reputed to have marched behind a bunch of heather tied to a pike.

MacDonnell of Glengarry's Regiment This joined the army at the Aberchalder rendezvous on 27 August 1745, and numbered as many as 400 men at Prestonpans, although this figure included 80 or more Grants of Glenmoriston and Glen Urquhart. Afterwards a small contingent of Macleods of Raasay were also included – as was, rather intermittently, a second battalion under Coll MacDonnell of Barisdale. The regiment was nominally commanded by Angus Og MacDonnell, younger of Glengarry, but he was largely employed at home and in practice it was led by Donald MacDonnell of Lochgarry, a sometime officer of the 64th Highlanders, who took full command after young Glengarry was accidentally shot at Falkirk. Still 500 strong at Culloden, the last remnant of the regiment was disbanded on or about 27 May 1746.

MacDonald of Keppoch's Regiment A small regiment with a sometimes unsavoury reputation for plundering and worse, commanded by Alexander MacDonald of Keppoch. Serving throughout the campaign,

ABOVE LEFT **Angus McDonnell, Glengarry's second son and commander of his regiment, was accidentally shot dead just after the battle of Falkirk. In the Penicuik sketch the sporran appears extravagantly large, but a very similar one can be seen in a more formal portrait of Major Fraser of Castle Leather.**
ABOVE RIGHT **Identified by the artist as 'Duncan McGregor of Dalnasplutrach', the original sketch actually appears under magnification to have been intended as a portrait of 'Donald McDonald of Cl...', which is probably a mistake for *Ranald MacDonald of Clanranald*. (Author's copies)**

Commit thy work to God

its strength averaged about 200 men, but these included the MacDonalds of Glencoe, the MacKinnons, and even some MacGregors as well as Keppoch's own clansmen. Keppoch was killed at Culloden, and the remains of the regiment were probably disbanded at Fort Augustus on or about 18 April 1746.

MacGregors Having been proscribed by successive governments since the beginning of the 17th century, the MacGregors' contribution to the Jacobite cause was somewhat fragmentary. At least two companies under James Mor Drummond/ MacGregor served in the Duke of Perth's Regiment; others under John MacGregor of Glengyle were attached to Keppoch's, and a third contingent led by MacGregor of Inverenzie served in Farquharson of Monaltrie's battalion of Lord Lewis Gordon's Regiment. Although there is some suggestion that the MacGregors may have formed a battalion of their own at Falkirk, it appears that they only acted independently at the end of the campaign when Glengyle was sent north in search of the French gold.

MacKinnon of MacKinnon's Regiment A small regiment from Skye commanded by John MacKinnon of MacKinnon, who 'raised near 4 score [80] of his own tenants, and marched as Colonel of them to Edinburgh'. On their arrival there he and his men were attached to Keppoch's Regiment, and remained with it until March 1746 when they were detached and sent north with Barisdale's men and the MacGregors.

Lady Mackintosh's Regiment Sometimes referred to in secondary sources as the Clan Chattan Regiment, this was a fairly large composite formation, not unlike the Atholl Brigade. It was raised in the Inverness area by Lady Mackintosh and commanded by Alexander McGillivray of Dunmaglass. Some 300 strong at Falkirk, and about 350 strong at Culloden, it was effectively destroyed there, losing most of its officers.

MacLachlans and MacLeans (see Plate A2). The former, commanded by Lachlan MacLachlan of Castle Lachlan, joined the Jacobite Army at the outset, as did a small company commanded by Captain John MacLean of Kingairloch. Although the two contingents were immediately combined they went through most of the campaign attached to Lord Nairne's Regiment of the Athole Brigade. Some time in March 1746 they were joined by a further contingent of MacLeans under Charles MacLean of Drimnin, and fought for the first time as an independent unit at Culloden, apparently with a strength of some 200 men commanded by MacLachlan with Drimnin as lieutenant-colonel.

Cluny MacPherson's Regiment Like MacDonnell of Lochgarry, Ewen MacPherson of Cluny a captain in Loudoun's 64th Highlanders at the outset of the Rising, but he and his company quickly changed sides and formed the nucleus of a regiment. This joined the Jacobite Army shortly after Prestonpans, took part in the English campaign, fought at Clifton Moor, and may have numbered as many as 400 officers and men at Falkirk. The regiment was not present at Culloden, and surrendered to the Earl of Loudoun on 17 May 1746. Cluny himself famously remained in hiding for many years before leaving for France in 1755.

Manchester Regiment (see Plate D3). Formed around a nucleus of English officers and men from the Duke of Perth's Regiment, this was originally to have been commanded by Captain Sir Francis Geohegan of the *Régiment Lally,* but for the sake of political expediency it was instead given to an Englishman, Francis Townley. The strength of the regiment never exceeded 300 men, of whom 118 were taken prisoner at Carlisle. Initially recruits were given blue and white ribbons formed into 'favours', but afterwards the rank and file were reported to have worn blue coats. At Townley's trial a witness named Roger MacDonald testified that the regiment's colours had the words *Liberty* and *Property* inscribed on one side, and *Church* and *Country* on the other. Unfortunately he failed to reveal what the colours actually looked like, but curiously enough an eyewitness to the Jacobites' arrival in Derby wrote that many of their regiments had white colours with red crosses. One of them was presumably the red saltire on a white field taken from an unidentified regiment at Culloden, but it is quite possible that the Manchester Regiment may have had a red cross of St George.

The blue colours of the 2nd Battalion of Lord Ogilvie's Regiment, still preserved in a Dundee museum; note that they are rectangular, not square.

No.4 on Wentworth's list was 'a blue silk colours, *Sursum Tendo*'. Interpreting this particular reference is not easy. It might be read to mean an otherwise plain blue field with a motto painted on it, but this would be very unusual, and it is more likely that the colour was simply identified by the motto since the arms were unrecognized. That motto uniquely belongs to the Kinloch family, which suggests that the colour was most likely that of Sir James Kinloch, who commanded the 2nd Battalion of Lord Ogilvie's Regiment. The arms are azure, a boar's head erased argent between three mascles or, with an eagle proper for a crest.

Moir of Stonywood's Battalion (see Plate C1). Raised in and around Aberdeen by James Moir of Stonywood in late 1745, this unit – unlike the other battalions of Lord Lewis Gordon's Regiment – was largely composed of volunteers. It fought at Inverurie on 23 December 1745, and afterwards at Falkirk and Culloden. The battalion was disbanded at Ruthven Barracks on 18 April 1746, and Ensign John Martin recalled seeing Stonywood tearing the colours from their staff there. These were presumably the same plain white colours carried by Lord Lewis Gordon's other battalions.

Lord Ogilvy's Regiment A large and well-disciplined unit raised in Forfarshire (now Angus) by David Lord Ogilvy, the eldest son of the Earl of Airlie. The first battalion, some 200 strong, joined the army at Edinburgh after Prestonpans, and served throughout the rest of the campaign. While the army was in England a second and larger battalion was raised by Sir James Kinloch, and elements of it took part in some scrappy fighting around Montrose and at Inverurie. Both battalions served together at Falkirk and Culloden, and after the army dispersed at Ruthven Barracks on 19 April 1746 continued home as a military unit, before eventually disbanding in Glen Clova on 21 April. Two colours associated with the second battalion are illustrated, one bearing a small white saltire in the centre and the other having the Kinloch arms.

Duke of Perth's Regiment (see Plate D1 and D2). Raised by James Drummond, Duke of Perth, in September 1745, this was perhaps the most representative of all the Jacobite regiments, since it variously included Highland and Lowland companies, English volunteers and former British Army personnel. Unsurprisingly, its organizational history was somewhat complex. About 200 men fought at Prestonpans, and thereafter it was considerably expanded, not only with volunteers raised in Edinburgh and from the remains of Cope's army, but also through the temporary addition of a second battalion.

This latter was a rather obscure unit formed from a number of companies raised by various individuals in Aberdeenshire and Banffshire, which arrived in Edinburgh during October 1745. Commenting on Jacobite activity in Aberdeen, a contemporary wrote: 'Mr [Robert] Sandilands raised a Company of Foot which joined them there, as also did two companies raised by Stonywood, the one commanded by himself, and the other by his brother [Charles Moir]; the whole not amounting to 200 men. These did indeed march south with Lord Pitsligo, but were afterwards incorporated in the Duke of Perth's second Battalion.' Other contingents were led by David Tulloch of Dunbennan and John Hamilton of Sandstoun, and the whole battalion numbered about 400 men. Exactly who commanded this second battalion is uncertain, since Stonywood and Dunbennan both returned home with Lord Lewis Gordon, and Sandstoun (who also had a commission to raise a troop of horse which was to have been styled the 'Scots Greys') became the Jacobite governor of Carlisle. Captain Robert Sandilands therefore seems the likeliest commander. Two companies were abandoned at Carlisle and on returning to Scotland the survivors were transferred or rather 'returned' to Avochie's and Stonywood's battalions of Lord Lewis Gordon's Regiment.

Since the Duke of Perth's Regiment was thus larger than most at the outset of the English campaign, three companies were re-assigned to the artillery. Perth then recruited a number of English Jacobites, only to have them taken to form the nucleus of the Manchester Regiment. After returning to Scotland, Perth's Regiment was not present at Falkirk, being assigned instead to blockade Stirling Castle; but it was about 200 strong at Culloden, where it was latterly posted on the extreme left of the front line.

Stewarts of Appin Some 200 men under Charles Stewart of Ardsheal joined the Jacobite Army at Invergarry on 29 August 1745, and served throughout the campaign. The unit was particularly prone to desertion; seemingly 350 strong at the outset of the march into England, they could only muster 300 men at Falkirk despite having been joined at Stirling by 150 fresh men under Alexander Stewart of Invernahyle. The unit was just 250 strong at Culloden; a return subsequently compiled by Ardsheal reveals that the regiment lost 90 killed and 65 wounded, though it is unclear whether this relates to Culloden alone or, as seems more likely, the whole campaign. A blue colour bearing a yellow saltire survives.

Colours carried by Ardsheal's Appin Regiment: a yellow saltire on blue. Despite their simplicity, these colours – which still survive – were no hasty improvisation; exactly the same ones are described by James Philip of Almericlose at the Dalcomera gathering in 1689.

John Roy Stuart's Regiment (see Plate C3). Also known as the Edinburgh Regiment, this was initially recruited in the city by Stuart, an experienced soldier who was a captain of grenadiers in the *Royal Écossois* at the time. Like the Duke of Perth's Regiment, it appears to have included for a time substantial numbers of former British Army personnel, 'but they mostly all left him'. The regiment took part in the march to Derby, but was not present at Falkirk, being assigned instead to blockade Stirling Castle. At Culloden it was about 200 strong, eventually standing in the front line next to the Stewarts of Appin. There is a tendency in secondary sources to dismiss the unit as being a rather poor one, but Captain Robert Stewart, who fought at Keith, commented that the detachment he commanded was assigned to the expedition because the regiment 'had a pretty good reputation'.

OTHER UNITS

Cavalry units

As for the much maligned cavalry, notwithstanding the popular but quite erroneous picture of small huddles of horseless troopers standing forlornly in the rear at Culloden, they actually represented a remarkable success story. Arguably their performance – at least when it came to scouting – was superior to that of their regular opponents. Furthermore, all of the Jacobite cavalry units remained mounted throughout the campaign except for Kilmarnock's and Lord Pitsligo's, who turned their horses over to the newly arrived *Fitzjames Cavallerie* in March 1746 and were then re-organized as a regiment of Footguards.

In organizational terms, it would appear that with the exception of the single troop of Hussars, each so-called regiment normally comprised two troops, albeit over-officered to an even greater degree than was the case in the infantry.

Scotch Hussars (see Plate E2). This unit, apparently comprising a single troop of about 50 men wearing tartan waistcoats and fur caps, was originally raised in Edinburgh by John Murray of Broughton, though it is unclear why it was designated as hussars. The caps were of an obsolete style once worn by hussars in the French Army, and may have been brought over from France (along with the blue coats turned up with red worn by the Lifeguards and the Manchester

A splendid illustration by Maclan of a Highland gentleman shown incongruously (but accurately) mounted upon a 'shelty' – what is now known as a Shetland Pony. Small though they were, these animals were often better at traversing rough and boggy ground than larger riding horses. In 1715 the Marquis of Huntly had a squadron of what he called 'light horse' mounted on such ponies, much to the amusement of everyone on both sides.

Among the most important of the Penicuik sketches are the only known contemporary images of one of the Scotch Hussars – see Plate E2. (Author's copy)

Regiment). Broughton himself served throughout the Rising on the Prince's staff, and the troop was initially led with no great distinction by a coterie of Lothian gentlemen headed by Captain George Hamilton of Redhouse. After Hamilton was captured at Clifton the troop was taken over by John Bagot, of the Irish *Régiment Rooth* (not, as is sometimes asserted, Matthew Bagot of *Fitzjames Cavallerie*), who turned it into an effective and notoriously raffish scouting unit which was apparently still 26 strong at Culloden. Although the unit was often referred to in secondary sources as 'Bagot's Hussars', a Jacobite cavalryman named Roger MacDonald, who served in Strathallan's, referred to them as the '*Scotch Hussars*'.

Lord Kilmarnock's Horse Why this unit, originally raised in West Lothian and Fife, was also designated as 'Horse Grenadiers' is unclear, and there are no suggestions in any eyewitness testimony that the men wore grenadier caps or any other distinctions to justify the title. It apparently comprised only one troop, but was brigaded, under Kilmarnock's command, with Lord Strathallan's Horse during the campaign in England. The troop was last mustered on 16 March 1746 and at that time comprised 1 quartermaster, 1 sergeant, 42 men and 8 recruits. Immediately afterwards it gave up its horses to mount *Fitzjames Cavallerie*, and formed the nucleus of a new regiment of Footguards.

Another, unfinished sketch of a hussar, this time armed with a straight-bladed broadsword rather than the sabre carried by the man in the finished illustration. Both men also have pistols, and although they are not shown here there is ample evidence that muskets were carried as well. (Author's copy)

Lifeguards (see Plate E3). Prince Charles Edward had a mounted lifeguard of sorts almost from the very beginning, but it was not properly formed until the army was at Edinburgh, at which time it may have numbered as many as 160 officers, gentlemen and servants, all wearing blue coats with red facings. Like most Jacobite cavalry units it comprised two troops, one commanded by Lord Elcho and the other by the Hon Arthur Elphinstone, who succeeded his elder brother as Lord Balmerino on 5 January 1746. Elcho's was very much the larger of the two troops, but by his own account it had dwindled to just 30 men at Culloden, while Balmerino's numbered just 16.

John Daniel, an English volunteer serving in Balmerino's troop, recorded that at Elgin it was given 'a curious fine standard with this motto *Britons Strike Home* that was taken at Falkirk from Gardiners [13th] Dragoons.' Unfortunately he did not describe it further, and British cavalry standards of this period are poorly documented; presumably it was green, the facing colour of the 13th, and swallow-tailed. Comparison of the few surviving examples of standards suggests that it probably had a small Union flag in the canton, and perhaps some kind of 'curious fine' device in the centre. Daniel carried it safely away from Culloden but it was afterwards lost when his riding coat, in which it had been stuffed, was stolen by two deserters from the Irish Picquets. (Oddly enough, they can be identified: Joseph and William Boes, two brothers from Westmeath, who had been serving in the *Royal Écossois* and *Régiment Rooth* respectively.)

Lord Pitsligo's Horse (see Plate E1). Originally raised in Aberdeenshire and some 130 strong, this unit served throughout most of the campaign, but was 'broke' at Elgin in March 1746 together with Lord Kilmarnock's troop; both were dismounted in order to provide sufficient horses for *Fitzjames Cavallerie*. Some of the officers and men may then have transferred to Moir of Stonywood's battalion, but most of them went into the Footguards.

Lord Strathallan's Horse Also known as the Perthshire Regiment, this was the first Jacobite cavalry troop to be raised, and was 36 strong at the battle of Prestonpans. Strathallan himself remained in Scotland as governor of Perth, so his men were temporarily brigaded with Lord

Sir William Gordon of Park (1712–51). A commission dated 18 October 1745 survives, appointing Park as lieutenant-colonel of Lord Pitsligo's Horse. After that unit was 'broken' at Elgin in March 1746, he may have transferred either to Lord Lewis Gordon's Regiment or to Lord Kilmarnock's Footguards. Eventually he escaped to France, and was there appointed lieutenant-colonel of the *Régiment d'Ogilvie*. Park is depicted here in gentleman's clothing, but John Gray remembered seeing him in 'a sort of highland clothing'. (Private Scottish collection)

Kilmarnock's during the campaign in England. A muster roll dated 7 February 1746 listed 82 officers and men in two troops, and as many as 70 of them were still mounted at Culloden, where Strathallan was killed. A breakdown of those appearing on the roll is interesting. Some 25 of them were gentlemen, identified either by the prefix 'Mr' or being described as 'of' a named place. Six others were professional men, chiefly lawyers, while another 20 were servants, presumably attending upon their gentlemen. The remainder were small tradesmen such as tailors, carpenters and shoemakers; there was a solitary labourer.

French officers and units

On 12 October 1745 a treaty was signed at Fontainebleau by the Marquis d'Argenson on behalf of King Louis XV and a Jacobite agent, Colonel O'Bryen, formally committing the French government to providing direct military assistance to the rebels.

The French auxiliaries serving with the Jacobite Army fell into two basic categories. As might be expected, professional assistance was not confined to the artillery, and a surprising number of individual officers acted as military advisers and instructors. The most important was

NEMO ME IMPUNE LACESSIT

The magnificent colours of the **Royal Écossois** featured gold *fleurs de lis* and a thistle displayed in its natural tinctures. Two colours were carried, the Regimental colour with a blue field and the King's with white.

Colonel John William Sullivan, a professionally trained staff officer who served as the army's Adjutant General and Quartermaster General and – notwithstanding a quite undeserved reputation as an incompetent – did so very efficiently (see below). Similarly, Colonel Sir John MacDonald of *Fitzjames Cavallerie* served as Inspector General of the Jacobite cavalry throughout the rising. At a lower level and perhaps more typical was the role played by Lieutenant Nicholas Glascoe of the *Régiment Dillon*, who was appointed major of the 2nd Battalion of Lord Ogilvy's Regiment. Inevitably, the majority of these military advisers belonged to the French Army's Irish Brigade, but others of Irish or Scottish descent included some exotics like Captain Jean O'Bryen of the Paris Militia, and Captain Charles Guilliame Douglas of the *Régiment Languedoc*.

Some of these officers were already serving more or less unofficially in Scotland before the signing of the treaty, and its most tangible result was the decision to send not only guns, ammunition and other supplies but regular troops as well. The first convoy, comprising three frigates and five Dunkirk privateers carrying two infantry battalions – Lord John Drummond's *Royal Écossois* and the famous Irish Picquets – sailed in mid-November 1745 under cover of a gale. Although two of the ships were intercepted by the Royal Navy, the bulk of Drummond's men were landed at Montrose on 26 November and others at Stonehaven and Peterhead. The relevant authorities were distracted for a time by the possibilities of mounting a full-scale invasion, and there were no further attempts to run the blockade until February 1746. The entire regiment *Fitzjames Cavallrie* was embarked at Ostend on 10 February, but only one of the three transports evaded the Royal Navy to land a squadron at Aberdeen on 22 February. In the meantime two more convoys were readied to carry 650 men of the regiments *Clare* and *Berwick* from Dunkirk, together with the whole of *Rooth* from Ostend. In the event the latter never sailed and most of the Dunkirk convoy was forced back, but a picquet of 46 men from *Berwick* was safely landed at Peterhead on 25 February.

None of these units were very large, but they proved to be an utterly reliable little force. They stood firm at Falkirk when everyone else (on both sides) was running away, and served as a sacrificial rearguard at Culloden. Had all of those shipped actually made it ashore the campaign might have taken on a different aspect. Even as it was, the arrival of the two little battalions in Scotland had the often overlooked dividend of forcing the withdrawal of a much larger Dutch contingent of ten battalions then serving with the British Army, which had earlier been captured at the fall of Tournai. The terms of their parole prevented them from serving against French troops or their auxiliaries – which the Jacobites had become by virtue of the Treaty of Fontaineblue.

Fitzjames Cavallerie (see Plate H3). Curiously enough, although designated as Irish and led by officers with Irish surnames, the troopers of this red-coated regiment – better known as Fitzjames's Horse – were substantially of English extraction, and included a surprising number of former merchant seamen. Ambitiously, it was intended to land the whole regiment in Scotland – which could have had interesting results, if achieved; but in the event 359 officers and men were captured at sea, and only a single squadron was landed at Aberdeen on 22 February 1746. Sullivan says that sufficient captured dragoon horses were found for 60 of them, but if so these must have been in very poor condition, since both Kilmarnock's and Pitsligo's regiments had to be dismounted in mid-March and their horses turned over. The Marquis d'Eguilles reported that the unit was 131 strong at Culloden, but it would appear that no more than half were mounted, so the remainder must have served on foot with the Irish Picquets.

Irish Picquets (see Plate G). Initially one picquet or detachment was embarked from each of the six Irish regiments in the French service. According to the 1750 regulations, which reflected established practice, a picquet was a sub-unit of company size comprising a captain, a lieutenant, two sergeants, a drummer and 47 men, all to be drawn from the fusilier or line companies of a regiment, although prisoner lists show that those sent to Scotland were double-officered. In the event only three of the picquets – drawn from the regiments *Dillon*, *Rooth* and *Lally* – actually made it to Scotland, where they were formed into a small provisional battalion. This served at Falkirk, the sieges of Fort Augustus and Fort William, and finally at Culloden. On the eve of the battle

Although actually depicting *Gardes Français* in 1752, these soldiers illustrated by Le Mire provide an excellent impression of the style of uniform worn by the Irish Picquets. Note the four-deep fighting line, apparently adopted by Jacobite units as well.

This French cavalry trooper, after a contemporary print, provides a good idea of the overall appearance of both Fitzjames's Horse and the Prince's Lifeguards. (Author's copy)

d'Eguilles reported that by then they had been reduced to a half, but had recruited 148 prisoners and deserters to bring their strength up to 260 men, to which should probably be added a further 60 or so dismounted troopers of *Fitzjames Cavallerie*.

Régiment Berwick (see Plate H2). No fewer than three picquets of this regiment were sent to Scotland at various times. The first was captured at sea, while the second landed at Peterhead at the end of February 1746 and served independently of the others until Culloden. According to d'Eguilles there were still 42 men on the strength at that battle, but Sullivan thought them much weaker, perhaps only 25 strong. The third picquet, serving as an escort for a shipment of £12,000 in gold, was forced ashore in the far north of Scotland on 25 March and forced to surrender to Loyalist militia the next day.

Compagnie Maurepas Not part of the French Army, this was a 'free company' made up of about 60 Franco-Irish volunteers and other assorted mercenaries. Recruited by Lord Clare, the commander of France's Irish Brigade, they were 'handsomely cloathed in blue faced with red'. In a contemporary history by James Ray they were intriguingly styled *Grassins de Mer*, presumably after the celebrated *Arquebusiers de Grassin*. If so, they may also have worn the cylindrical mirleton caps or shakos generally associated with French light troops rather than conventional three-cornered hats. At any rate, the Prince himself admitted that they were simply intended to make a show in the highlands – 'they having a pretty uniform' – and so to create at least an illusion of French assistance. In the event their only service was in the sea fight with HMS *Lion*, in which they lost seven dead before being carried back to France aboard the crippled *L'Elisabeth*.

Royal Écossois (see Plate F). This was a single-battalion regiment formed in 1744 around a cadre drawn from various Irish regiments in French service, although there is some evidence that efforts were made to raise a second battalion while it was in Scotland. The regiment was transported there entire, and was lucky to lose only 60 officers and men en route when *L'Esperance* was captured off the Dogger Bank. The bulk of the regiment landed at Montrose on 26 November 1745, and a detachment subsequently fought at Inverurie on 23 December. The

(continued on page 41)

THE CLANS
1: Alexander Grant younger of Shewglie
2: Highland clansman
3: Highland clansman wearing plaid

A

LORD LEWIS GORDON'S REGIMENT
1: Col Francis Farquharson of Monaltrie
2: Maj David Tulloch of Dunbennan
3: Volunteer, John Gordon of Avochie's Bn

B

LOWLAND INFANTRY
1: James Moir of Stonywood's Bn
2: James Crichton of Auchingoul's Bn
3: John Roy Stuart's Regt

C

DUKE OF PERTH'S REGIMENT
1: 'Redcoat'
2: Major James Stewart
3: Manchester Regiment

D

CAVALRY
1: Lord Pitsligo's Horse
2: Scotch Hussars
3: Volunteer, Prince's Lifeguard

E

ROYAL ÉCOSSOIS
1 & 1a: Officer of Grenadiers
2: Piper
3: Fusilier

F

IRISH PICQUETS
1: Fusilier, *Régiment Dillon*
2: Fusilier, *Régiment Lally*
3: Officer, *Régiment Rooth*

G

OTHER IRISH TROOPS
1: 'Volunteer', Guise's (6th) Foot
2: Fusilier, *Régiment Berwick*
3: Trooper, *Fitzjames Cavallerie*

H

grenadier company and a fusilier picquet were at Falkirk, and according to d'Eguilles the regiment was still some 350 strong shortly before Culloden. There it was commanded by Lieutenant-Colonel Lord Lewis Drummond of Melfort, subsequently surrendering at Inverness on 19 April. Its magnificent colours, bearing a large thistle displayed on a saltire, are illustrated.

The artillery

The Jacobite artillery was not quite the ill-assorted assemblage of guns, mismatched ammunition and untrained gunners so often represented. In charge of the artillery for much of the campaign was Colonel James Grant, a well-regarded officer in the French service, who organized at Edinburgh a little battalion formed from two companies of the Duke of Perth's Regiment acting as gunners and a third serving as pioneers. It was originally intended that the latter were to be drawn from those members of the Duke of Perth's who were 'gardeners, carpenters and other workmen to serve as Pioneers and to march at the head of the Artillery'; in the event Captain James Johnstone's company appears to have been assigned to the task, together with a detachment from the Manchester Regiment. One of the actual artillery companies, left behind at Carlisle, was commanded by Captain John Burnet of Campfield, who had once 'belonged to the Artillery company at Woolwich'. He was not the only professional gunner: Grant had brought 12 French gunners with him in October to serve as instructors, and two French artillery officers named d'Andrion and Bodin were amongst those who surrendered after Culloden, together with an engineer officer named Du Saussey who had commanded a gun there. The management of the artillery was therefore not quite so amateurish as is sometimes portrayed.

The cannon themselves were mostly British pieces, either small, obsolete guns captured from General Cope's army at Prestonpans, or more modern ones taken by the French at Fontenoy and run through the blockade. Inevitably they were of various calibres, but the 11 guns deployed at Culloden – the only occasion when artillery was used on the battlefield – were all 3-pounders, so whatever their failings that day, confusion caused by a multiplicity of calibres was not one of them.

Nevertheless, over the few short months of its existence the Jacobite Army did find itself encumbered with a quite surprising variety of pieces. Some swivel guns were landed from the *Le du Teillay*, but these lacked carriages of any kind – although there was a proposal to mount them in 'sleeping batteries' (i.e. simply to lay the barrels on the ground) in hopeful anticipation of Cope's trying to force the Corryairack Pass. It was not until they invaded England that the Jacobites could boast a proper artillery train. According to Colonel Grant, who should have known what he was talking about, this comprised 'thirteen pieces, six whereof were taken from Sir John Cope, six 4-pounders that came from France, [and] one piece that was brought from Blair of Atholl'. Cope's guns were brass 1½-pdr curricle guns, so called because the barrel was mounted on a light flat-bottomed cart or curricle whose shafts doubled as the trail. The 4-pdrs, confusingly enough, were also known as 'Swedish' guns, not because they were Swedish in origin but because they were an experimental light iron-barrelled type, inspired by if not copied from

The plaid worn in bad weather – another MacIan painting, illustrating how clansmen could sometimes look like untidy bundles of washing on legs. The larger, flat bonnet seems to have been more characteristic of Lowland rather than Highland Scotland.

the light artillery employed by Gustavus Adolphus a century before. The last piece Grant mentions, described as an 'octagon' when it was found abandoned at Carlisle, must have been an old brass gun dating back to the 16th century, when such octagonal barrels were in vogue.

A number of guns appear to have been left at Carlisle, although the 4-pdrs at least were brought back. In the meantime, on 24 November, the *Le Renommée* landed a small siege train at Montrose comprising two 18-pdrs, two 12-pdrs and two 9-pdrs. In addition another blockade runner landed a number of British 3-pdrs which had earlier been taken at Fontenoy, while another of these useful pieces was subsequently captured at Falkirk. The big guns were abandoned when the army retreated further north, but there were still 22 assorted guns and 8 swivels at the end. It is clear from John Finlayson's map that only 11 guns, all 3-pdrs, were actually deployed on the moor at the outset of Culloden, and one other – probably a 'Swedish' 4-pdr – was brought up by the French engineer Du Saussey after the battle had begun.

Assessments of what these guns actually achieved tend to be

excessively coloured by their perceived poor performance at Culloden, and by the fact that they never came into action at all at Falkirk – yet as General Hawley remarked on that occasion, for an army to march without artillery would have been 'silly'. In reality, away from the battlefield the Jacobite artillery actually proved its worth on a number of occasions. At Fort Augustus a French engineer dropped a mortar bomb squarely on to the fort's magazine, which was not only vastly discouraging to the garrison but also succeeded in demolishing the bastion in which it was situated, and so brought about an immediate surrender. They were less lucky at Fort William, but the successful defence of that important post was solely due to the tenacity of the garrison, for it was quite literally shot to pieces around them. Although Lord George Murray failed to take Blair Castle because neither of his guns was heavy enough (and one obstinately refused to shoot straight), the mere display of artillery was sufficient to persuade the redoubtable Sergeant Terry Molloy to surrender Ruthven Barracks.

Against the Royal Navy the Prince's artillery also had some success. French and Jacobite gunners trapped HMS *Hazard* in Montrose harbour long enough for the tide to recede, leaving her stranded and helpless; while batteries at Elphinstone Pans and Alloa on the lower reaches of the Forth prevented interference with Jacobite operations around Stirling.

All in all, while the artillery was never effective in a Napoleonic sense, it was a useful tool. There is no doubt that notwithstanding the effort expended in moving it around, the Jacobite Army would have had a much poorer time without it.

The train

The same could not be said of the train. Accustomed to being sent overseas on crowded transports with limited hold space, the British Army had long since learned to rely on pack horses. Similarly, Jacobite orderly books note that each company had or should have had two each, 'and their proportion of tents, etc', besides the officers' servants with their cloak-bags. In fact the Jacobite baggage train was very largely improvised, using a mixture of country carts and heavy four-wheeled wagons. The orderly books refer variously to baggage wagons, ammunition wagons and carts, bread wagons and (when leaving Glasgow), 'Carts with the Clothing of the Foot'. All of these quickly proved too slow and unsuitable for the poor roads over which the campaign was fought. Those, including Captain Johnstone, who struggled to get the wagons over Shap Fell never forgot the awful experience, and in the end the train even proved unequal to hauling food out from Inverness to the army in the days before Culloden.

LEADERSHIP AND ADMINISTRATION

In addition to their infantry, cavalry, artillery and trains, the Jacobites also boasted another essential component of a modern 18th century army: a surprisingly sophisticated staff organization. This was essentially the creation of the much-maligned Irishman Colonel Sullivan, whose competence has long been obscured by his feud with one of the army's Scottish lieutenant-generals, Lord George Murray.

Lord George Murray (1694–1760). James Johnstone noted that although possessed of 'an infinity of good qualities', he was also 'proud, haughty, blunt and imperious'.

The term 'lieutenant general' was employed in the Jacobite Army in its literal sense, denoting one of the Prince's lieutenants or subordinates rather than as a definite hierarchical rank. There were initially three: the Duke of Athole, alias Tullibardine; his younger brother, Lord George Murray, and the Duke of Perth. None of them were professional soldiers, and the first was so old as to be incapable of serving in the field. In the early days there was an understanding that Murray and Perth should command on alternate days; but while the army was in England,

An alternative view of Murray by the Victorian artist Robert Mclan, which probably gives a fair impression of his appearance at Falkirk, where he chose to fight on foot; Mclan shows the jacket as a drab 'hodden grey' with gold lace, the waistcoat and garters red. However, the 19th-century sett shown here – Murray of Atholl – is quite different from the only known portrait of him wearing tartan. Note the Murray field sign of a sprig of broom in his blue bonnet, together with eagle feathers.

Perth was prevailed upon to stand down since he was a Roman Catholic, and placing him at the head of the army would therefore be politically disastrous to any hopes of raising significant support in England. Murray thus enjoyed a considerable ascendancy for a time; but then Perth's brother, Lord John Drummond, arrived from France.

This immediately altered the balance of power, for – as even one of his own aides-de-camp admitted – 'Lord George was vigilant, active, and diligent; his plans were always judiciously formed, and he carried them promptly and vigorously into execution. However, with an infinity of good qualities, he was not without his defects: proud, haughty, blunt and imperious, he wished to have the exclusive disposal of everything and, feeling his superiority, would listen to no advice.' This attitude did not sit well with many of his colleagues, particularly the MacDonalds. He was also distrusted by many on account of a somewhat chequered past, and from Drummond's arrival onwards his influence was considerably weakened.

In any case the three officers – Murray and the two Drummond brothers – were in effect little more than the equivalent of brigade commanders, and consequently the overall direction of the army increasingly devolved upon Murray's nemesis, Colonel Sullivan. With the Prince no more than a passive spectator, to all intents and purposes it was Sullivan who was left in operational command of the army at Falkirk and Culloden.

James Drummond, Duke of Perth (1713–47). Overshadowed throughout the campaign by his fellow lieutenant-general, Lord George Murray, Perth nevertheless proved a reasonably competent commander, and was far more popular within the army. His clothing as depicted here is typical of senior Jacobite officers, although the plaid is draped in classical fashion for effect rather than utility. (Private Scottish collection)

Hailing from County Kerry, the 40-year-old John William Sullivan (or O'Sullivan) was a captain on the French *État Major* when he was recruited by Lord Clare to accompany Prince Charles Edward to Scotland. Colonel Sir John McDonnell recalled:

'At the raising of the standard Locheil said to me that never having had the opportunity of seeing armies, he knew little of military affairs, but would take council of those of us who had experience of such matters. I therefore told him that the first thing to do was appoint a second in command to see to the details of guards, marches etc and to avoid confusion; that I was sure Mr Sulivan was as competent a man for this purpose as could be found anywhere, because I had known him in the Italian wars. That if he had not been there, [Colonel Francis] Strickland or I could have done the job, which is a most essential one, but that Sulivan could do it much better. I also spoke of it to HRH, who agreed... Two or three days passed and nothing was done. I therefore took the liberty of suggesting to HRH to carry out the plan, otherwise his army would be in confusion and disorder. The Prince approving, I called upon Sulivan to write out an order for the detaching of guards, as he thought fit, in order to instal himself as Adjutant General, which was done...'.

In fact Sullivan also took on the role of Quartermaster General as well, a post which in the 1740s had nothing to do with supplies and everything to do with the movement and 'quartering' or deploying of the army. One of the Jacobite Army's greatest strengths was its ability to conduct rapid marches, and often to do so in dispersed columns. This was sometimes done for tactical reasons, but more often to make the best use of a rudimentary road network and to ensure that sufficient shelter could be found for the troops in the often bad weather in which the army operated. James Johnstone's description of the Jacobite march on Carlisle is striking:

'Our army was formed into three columns, each of which took a separate road when setting out from Dalkeith... hardly any person in our army had the least idea of the place where the junction of the three columns would take place, and we were very much surprised on finding ourselves all arrive on the 9th of November, almost at the same instant, on a heath in England, about a mile from the town of Carlisle. This march was arranged and executed with such precision that there was not an interval of two hours between the arrival of the different columns.'

Sullivan's march tables, so necessary to achieve this, represented staff work of the highest order, which contrasted sharply with the rather headlong leadership style favoured by Murray. A similar attention to practical detail is evident in the surviving regimental orderly books; however, Murray complained that Sullivan's system was all very well for regular armies, but that instead of simply assuming that orders would be obeyed it was necessary to relay them personally. Coming from an officer who was himself quite incapable of following any kind of orders, this was a little rich, and ignores the fact that commanding an army is very different from leading a company or even a regiment.

In the early days of the Rising the Jacobite orderly books certainly abound with weary comments deploring the fact that 'the Majors, or some others acting for them, are not more punctual in the Execution of their orders'; and Sir John McDonnell dryly noted that old Glenbuchat 'was the only Scot I ever knew who was able to start off at the hour fixed'. Nevertheless, once the army left Edinburgh a much more professional attitude was evident, as was a recognition of the importance of training.

WEAPONS

Glascoe and the other Irish officers from the French service at first bitterly resented being 'forced to discipline the Militia', but they quickly found a receptive audience. It should be emphasized that the Jacobite Army was no mere wolfpack of Highland swordsmen.

In fact, although some 2,000 cheap broadswords were carried from France aboard the *Le du Teillay*, swords generally appear to have been in surprisingly short supply. One much quoted observer in Edinburgh declared that the men who took the city in September 1745 had 'guns of different syses, and some of innormows length, some with butts turned up lick a heren, some tyed with puck threed to the stock, some withowt locks and some matchlocks, some had swords over ther showlder instead of guns, one or two had pitchforks, and some bits of sythes upon poles with a cleek [hook], some old Lochaber axes'. This sorry picture did not last very long, however – the victory at Prestonpans saw to that.

Most of the clansmen depicted in an important series of eye-witness sketches by an unknown artist from Penicuick, near Edinburgh, are indeed carrying or brandishing the swords with which they are still popularly associated, and it is true that contemporary commentators on both sides wrote as if all or most had them. On the other hand, closer investigation reveals a rather different picture. Returns of weapons seized or surrendered in the months after Culloden actually included comparatively few broadswords. When, for example, 19 men from Glen Urquhart and 68 from Glenmoriston surrendered to the Laird of Grant at Balmacaan on 5 May 1746, they handed over a total of 69 firelocks, 7 bayonets, 7 pistols, 34 swords, 4 dirks and one Lochaber axe. Similarly, when a further 77 of Glengarry's men surrendered on 15 May they handed over 65 firelocks but only 26 swords and 4 dirks.

There is, of course, a lively possibility that some men had chosen to conceal their swords; but this cannot cancel out the evidence from Culloden Moor itself. The generally accepted estimate is that up to 1,500 Jacobites may have been killed or wounded there, and at least 750 were certainly counted lying dead on the battlefield; yet when it was cleared, only 190 broadswords were recovered. This must mean that at best only one in four of those killed or wounded on

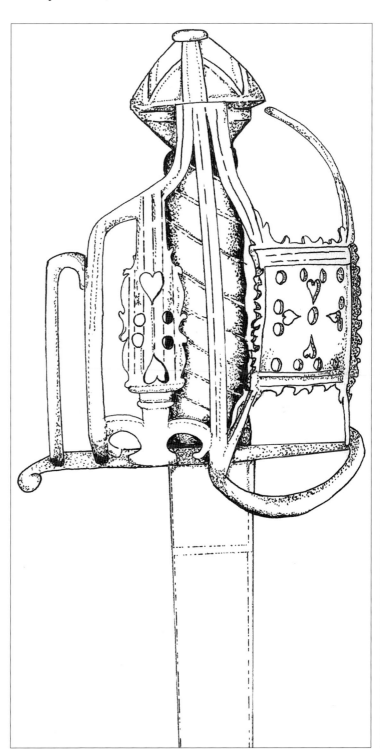

The weapon most commonly associated with the Jacobites was the basket-hilted broadsword, of which this is a typical example with a Glasgow-made hilt.

A fine rear view of a Highland soldier wearing the belted plaid and apparently armed only with a firelock and bayonet. (Author's copy)

the moor itself was carrying a broadsword at the time. This would have been sufficient for each of those standing in the front rank – the Highland gentlemen; but their followers in consequence must have been relying upon their firelocks and bayonets. This was in fact graphically illustrated not only by the Penicuik sketches, but also by the discovery of a French bayonet in the area where the clans impacted on the British front line at Culloden, during archaeological excavations by a team from Glasgow University in 2005.

There may also have been a similar shortage of the round shields called targes. The named Highland gentlemen in the sketches generally carry them, but not the rank and file. On 30 September 1745 the city of Edinburgh was ordered to provide 2,000 'targets' for the army; since most of the Lowland regiments had yet to come in at that time, this indicates that even the clansmen at Prestonpans were lacking them, and that they were perhaps being ordered to complement the cheap French broadswords brought over by the Prince. How many were actually delivered is not known, although Lord Ogilvy ordered 'that all the Officers of his Regiment provide themselves in Targets from the armorers in Edinburgh'. The likelihood is that for the most part targes – perhaps like the Prince's imported broadswords – were regarded by ordinary Jacobite soldiers as an encumbrance rather than an asset, just as a later generation of Black Watch soldiers 'declined using broadswords', preferring to rely on bayonets instead. Even those who did carry targes seem to have thrown most of them away on the night march which preceded the battle of Culloden.

In fact, as both documentary evidence and those invaluable Penicuick sketches reveal, all Jacobite soldiers were eventually armed with modern firelocks, and usually with bayonets as well. The orderly books are full of routine injunctions to officers and NCOs requiring them to ensure that their men's arms were 'well fixed' and in good order, and it is clear that their firelocks rather than their swords were regarded as their primary weapons.

As to the preferred type, many no doubt brought a bewildering variety of fowling pieces, blunderbusses and other individually owned guns of all kinds and in all conditions when they first joined the army; but sufficient Land Pattern firelocks were certainly gleaned from the field of Prestonpans to completely equip Glenbuchat's and Lord Ogilvy's newly raised regiments, as well as uncounted

An interesting sketch by the Penicuik artist depicting a man armed with both a so-called Lochaber axe and an old sword, or perhaps a hanger. As he is clearly wearing rather ragged breeches rather than Highland dress, it is just possible that he is a member of the Duke of Perth's Regiment, which was at first very badly armed. (Author's copy)

individuals. In addition, in October 1745 alone some 2,500–2,600 stand of French muskets were run through the blockade and landed at Montrose and Stonehaven. More followed over the next few months; a cargo of 2,500 Spanish weapons (which shared the same .69in calibre) was landed in Barra in October or November 1745, and a second in Peterhead in late January 1746. Consequently, by early 1746 the Jacobites must have been able to standardize their primary weapons to a significant degree. After Culloden, Ensign Stewart of Lascelles' (58th/47th) Regiment was ordered to draw 'French or Spanish firelocks and bayonets and cartridge boxes' from the train and to 'distribute them to the prisoners of our army released here'. Clearly, by that time there were not many captured British firelocks amongst the arms recovered from the battlefield.

The position on cartridge boxes is less clear, however, and those delivered to Ensign Stewart may only have been those taken from the French regulars, for while it cannot be ruled out, there is no actual evidence of their being carried by ordinary Jacobite soldiers. On the contrary, in telling of his part in the fight at Keith a rebel captain named Robert Stewart related the farcical scene when he decided at the last minute that it would be prudent to inspect the 50-man detachment assigned to him, and found their arms and ammunition 'in a very indifferent order [and] was obliged to dispense most of his own powder and shot (who kept himself well provided on all occasions)'. Presumably they simply carried it in their pockets. Sometimes ammunition was

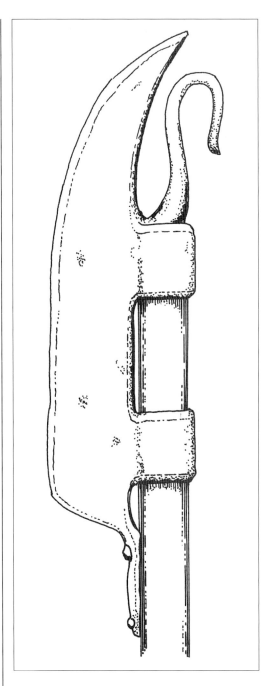

The so-called Lochaber axe was not a specialist weapon, but rather a cheap substitute carried by those men lacking either broadsword or firelock. Any blacksmith could make one; some hundreds were hastily manufactured in Aberdeen in late 1715 for equipping the Earl of Mar's levies, and some are still seen in the Penicuik sketches from 1745.

issued in the form of ready-made cartridges, and there is a single note in the orderly books for Lord Ogilvy's Regiment for 3 November 1745 that every man was 'to have 12 shot' (a pretty average ammunition scale for European armies at this period). Stewart's reference to 'powder and shot' clearly suggests that ordinarily they may have used powder flasks and carried the balls loose in their pockets or their sporrans.

TACTICS

For the most part those men who did have broadswords stood in the front ranks, and despite his disdainful view of the bulk of the rebels there is no reason to disbelieve General Hawley's description of this practice: 'They Commonly form their Front rank of what they call their best men, or True Highlanders, the number of which being always but few, when they form in Battallions they commonly form four deep, & these Highlanders form the front of the four, the rest being lowlanders & arrant scum.' In another frequently quoted passage, James Johnstone summed up Highland fighting methods thus:

'Their manner of fighting is well adapted for brave but undisciplined men. They advance with rapidity, discharge their pieces when within musket-length of the enemy, and then, throwing them down, draw their swords, and holding a dirk in their left hand with their target, dart with fury on the enemy through the smoke of their fire… The reason assigned by the Highlanders for their custom of throwing their muskets on the ground is not without its force. They say they embarrass [hamper] them in their operations, even when slung behind them, and on gaining a battle, they can pick them up again along with the arms of their enemies; but, if they should be beaten, they have no [further] occasion for muskets.'

However, those following behind the swordsmen could do little more than swell the numbers, and Sullivan took a rather less sanguine view in describing these tactics: 'Any man that served with Highlanders, knows that they fire but one shot, abandon their firelocks after. If there be any obstruction that hinders them from going on the enemy, all is lost; they don't like to be exposed to the enemy's fire, nor can they resist it, not being trained to charge [i.e. reload] as fast as regular troops, especially the English, which are the troops in the world that fires best.'

Although Johnstone went on to describe cheerfully just what the front-rank men could do with their broadswords and dirks, actually engaging in hand-to-hand combat was rare: the success of a Highland charge depended on their intimidating the enemy before actually making contact. It was indeed the Highland gentlemen who won the

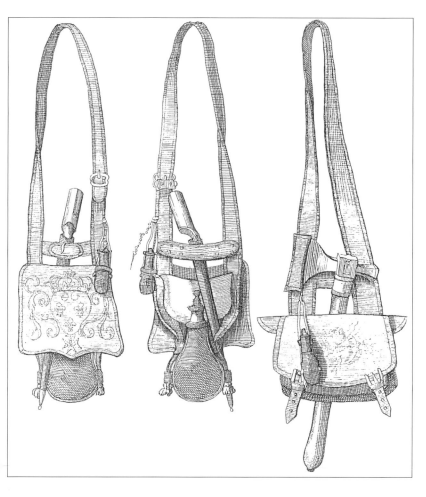

These French infantry equipments illustrated in Saint-Remy's *Memoires d'artillerie* (1697) would have been obsolete by 1745, but some may have been included in the miscellany of old equipment off-loaded on the Jacobites. Despite having the outward appearance of a cartridge box or *giberne*, the equipment on the left actually comprises a large powder flask, a small powder flask for priming, and a bullet bag. The equipment on the right is a satchel for carrying grenades – grenadiers carried their ammunition as made-up cartridges in a *gargousier* or belly-box.

battle of Prestonpans, by brandishing their broadswords menacingly in a headlong rush which frightened the life out of Cope's raw Scots recruits, brought up as they had been on folk tales and memories of Highland ferocity. If, on the other hand, the defending troops held their nerve and stood firm, the Highlanders were often reluctant to close with them at all.

This is clearly illustrated by what happened at Culloden. Due to a combination of factors the Jacobite right-wing units became jammed together in a solid uncontrollable mass, which impacted on the British Army's left flank and overran Barrell's 4th Foot through sheer weight of numbers; but the clansmen were then halted by a counter-attack and were literally decimated in a very unequal firefight shot out at point-blank range. The Jacobite left wing, on the other hand, slowed by boggy ground, advanced much more deliberately and then finally came to a halt well short of the British front line. 'They came down three several times within a hundred yards of our men,' wrote one British officer, 'firing their pistols and brandishing their swords; but our brave soldiers appeared as if they took little notice of their bravado.' Baffled by the soldiers' failure to run away, the Highlanders hesitated to advance further.

There was nothing unusual in this: most other European soldiers tacitly halted before actually colliding with their opponents, and then commenced firing on each other until one side or the other gave

way. The problem, of course, as Sullivan pointed out, was that once this happened the Jacobites were simply not well enough trained or equipped to shoot it out on equal terms.

Culloden was by no means the exception to the rule – if anything, Prestonpans was the untypical encounter – and when those tactics produced less spectacular results on the rain-soaked hillside at Falkirk four months after Prestonpans, the chiefs were in no doubt about the reason, as Lord George Murray himself explained:

'…[The] best of the Highland officers, whilst they remained at Falkirk after the battle, were absolutely convinced, that, except they could attack the enemy at a very considerable disadvantage, either by surprise or by some strong situation of ground, or a narrow pass, they could not expect any great success, especially if their numbers were no ways equal, and that a body of regular troops was absolutely necessary to support them, when they should at any time go in, sword in hand; for they were sensible, that without more leisure and time to discipline their own men, it would not be possible to make them keep their ranks, or rally soon enough upon any sudden emergency, so that any small number of the enemy, either keeping in a body when they were in confusion, or rallying, would deprive them of a victory…'

It would be hard to find a clearer analysis of exactly what went wrong for the Jacobites at Falkirk and Culloden; and it is interesting to find frequent references to even the clan regiments being drilled and 'disciplined' in the later stages of the campaign. In fact there is evidence enough that this had been going on right from the very beginning. Lord Ogilvy, for example, ordered that 'the Serjeants be careful to cause the men keep their arms clean, and qualify themselves for learning the men their Exercise.' Unfortunately it is not at all clear exactly what that exercise was. As it happens, one of Ogilvy's men, John Webster from Forfar, was a Chelsea out-pensioner who 'Taught the Rebels the Exercise of the Firelock', which would suggest that initially at least some of them were trained according to the British Army's 1727 *Regulations* as devised by Humphrey Bland. On the other hand, Lord George Murray is sometimes credited with devising a simplified drill better suited to Highlanders, but little is known of what it actually comprised, although Johnstone does give an indication of just how rudimentary it was:

'The Highlanders have a very simple manoeuvre well suited to a small army composed of undisciplined men. They formed themselves in line, three deep, and by facing to the right or left, they formed

This illustration by the Penicuik artist is atypical in being a battle scene, probably depicting either Prestonpans or Falkirk – he has carefully indicated the allegiance of the Jacobites' dead enemies (see right foreground). The sketch offers much of interest, including the piper, and the way the central figure's plaid is worn like a blanket roll – a feature seen in other sketches. (Author's copy)

themselves into a column for marching, three men in front; and in the same manner, by facing to right or left, they were instantly in order of battle. It was deemed more advisable to allow them to adhere to their ancient and simple manoeuvre, than to teach them, imperfectly, the more complicated movements of wheeling backwards to form columns of division, sub-division etc and afterwards to form into line.'

It may have been easy, but it was also a very clumsy way of manoeuvring, and the advent of French Army instructors such as Nicholas Glascoe soon saw the introduction of proper training, not just for the Lowland regiments but for the Highlanders as well, and the adoption of French practices. Contemporary French tactical doctrines, calling for rapid movements in column formation, and an emphasis on shock tactics rather than firepower, were actually well suited to the Jacobites. So was their practice of firing an initial series of volleys by ranks and then if necessary continuing the fight with a *feu à billebaude* – which essentially meant each man loading and blazing away in his own time. Once again, this was something which was far easier to teach raw 'militia' than the complicated platoon firing practiced by the British Army.

Consequently, the French influence is clearly to be seen in the initial dispositions at Culloden. With the exception of the Atholl Brigade, the front line was at first entirely comprised of clan regiments, drawn up not three deep as described by Johnstone, but in four ranks after the French fashion, just as they had been at Falkirk. The difference at Culloden was that the Lowland regiments did not form an extended second line, but were deployed in column formation in the centre under John Roy Stuart, as a powerful reserve ready to move swiftly to wherever they might be needed. These columns were fairly solid tactical formations with a frontage of one or perhaps two companies rather than just three men, and in order to fight they had to be able to

One of McIan's most dramatic reconstructions shows the death at Culloden of Major Gillies McBean of Lady Mackintosh's Regiment. He is shown wearing a short blue jacket turned up with red, over a white waistcoat with floral embroidery.

deploy from those columns by company or division [paired companies] rather than simply by facing to right or left in some 'ancient' fashion. To do that required proper drill training.

In the event the effectiveness of that training was never really put to the test, since nearly all of the regiments forming the reserve were steadily bled away before the battle even started, either to fill gaps in the front line, or afterwards to form a defensive line in the right rear against an outflanking move by the British cavalry. Consequently, when the Highland charge stalled and the 'emergency' predicted by Murray and the chiefs arose, only two battalions (the *Royal Écossois* and Kilmarnock's newly formed Footguards) were left in the reserve, and although they gamely came forward to deliver a token volley they could do nothing to influence the outcome of the battle.

BOTH **In marked contrast to the many blood-chilling Highland swordsmen illustrated by the Penicuik artist are a number of less warlike figures, perhaps representing wounded men and stragglers left behind when the Jacobites abandoned Edinburgh. (Author's copies)**

AFTERWARDS

The Jacobite Army was famously defeated at Culloden Moor, outside Inverness, on 16 April 1746. In all the circumstances the rebels made a far better fight of it than their leaders or anyone else had a right to expect, and afterwards a significant portion of the army got away in tolerably good order. The outcome had never really been in doubt, however, and the decision to disband the remaining regiments two days later was simply realistic.

At that point the *Royal Écossois* returned to Inverness to join the Irish Picquets and the other French troops already in captivity, and there to await their eventual exchange; but their rebel colleagues fared rather differently. At the first count there were 154 prisoners in Inverness, many of them 'terribly wounded', besides another 172 of Cromartie's men captured the day before Culloden. More soon followed, and with those already sitting in jails up and down the country it has been reckoned that from first to last some 3,471 were held. That figure is in fact considerably inflated by some double counting; by the inclusion of many, but not all of the French prisoners of war; by civil and military prisoners who had not actually served in the Jacobite Army; and by a number of non-combatants. Whatever the true total, it was still more than enough to overwhelm the ordinary criminal justice system, and

Fix them, and Recover; 3 Mo:

Front Ranks push your Bayonets 3 times 6 Mo:

Front .... ranks stand, fast as you are, Rear ranks march 3 paces in a line as you stand, center D.? First draw up your left foot to y.? right heel, count 3 & 2 with y.? right foot, At y.? Word of command turn your Firelock as lightning over your left Arm Seizing y.? Butt & extending y.? right foot a little further in a line w.th y.? left y.? Rear ranks seizing y.? Cocks, as they turn over y.? left Arm, keeping their Elbows high to clear y.? front rank

radical measures were employed to deal with them all.

Exclusive of former British Army personnel found wearing French or Jacobite uniforms, a total of 73 men were executed for treason, representing a complete cross-section of every rank from regimental commanders – such as Lord Kilmarnock and Francis Townley – down to ordinary clansmen. A further 936 were either sentenced to transportation to the colonies, or else allowed to volunteer for it in preference to the uncertainty of a trial. However, an astonishing 700–800 prisoners were unceremoniously drafted into the ranks of the British Army. On 31 July 1746, no fewer than 250 rebel prisoners were taken for Dalzell's long-suffering 38th Foot on Antigua; 100 more were ordered for Trelawney's 63rd on Jamaica, and 200 apiece for Shirley's and Pepperell's American regiments at Cape Breton. A year later, others were more or less press-ganged into the Independent Companies raised to go with Admiral Boscawen to India – and some of them even returned.

Of those who got away, some obviously entered the French Army, either in the ranks of the *Royal Écossois* or in one of the other two 'Scottish' regiments – *Ogilvy* and *Albanie* – raised in the aftermath of the Rising. Nevertheless, a surprising number chose instead to seek their fortune in the service of King George or the East India Company. None managed the leap quite so adroitly as Simon Fraser, sometime Master of Lovat, who began his career as a colonel in the Jacobite Army and finished it a lieutenant-general in the British Army.

BOTH **Highland soldier fixing his bayonet, and performing bayonet drill, in illustrations from George Grant's *New Highland Military Discipline* of 1757; although they appeared a decade after the '45, the figures belong to that earlier period. Despite the neck stock and the vague hint of a waist pouch marked 'GR', the jackets may not even be military – the braiding down the front edges was a civilian fashion. Whatever the true origin of these sketches, and despite their relative crudity, they provide a fair picture of the general appearance of many Jacobite soldiers at the time of the Rising.**

PLATE COMMENTARIES

A: THE CLANS

The Jacobite decision to present themselves as the 'Highland army' was a pragmatic one, which immediately gave them a real sense of identity and also opened the way to providing them with a very distinctive uniform. From the very beginning every effort was made to dress the army in tartans. In October 1745, for example, the Earl of Cromartie and his son were noted to be engaged in 'preparation such as the making of Highland clothes', while Lord Lewis Gordon similarly demanded that men levied out for his regiment should be dressed in plaids. This required bulk purchases and requisitions, such as the 6,000 coats and waistcoats demanded from the authorities in Glasgow, as well as those acquired at a more local level. This must have led to a great deal more uniformity in some Lowland companies than in 'real' Highland units; it must be

ABOVE **Inverness marketplace, as depicted by Edward Burt in the 1730s. The heavily armed man in the centre is presumably a soldier of the Black Watch, but the other figures are also of interest; in particular, the man on the extreme left should be compared with Plate A2.**

BELOW **Although crude, this unusual illustration in Burt's _Letters from the North of Scotland_ shows how Highlanders dressed in wintry weather – see Plate A3. Three of the four are wearing trews, and two are also wearing belted plaids. The figure second from right appears to be wearing a rather long tartan coat and a plaid as well as his trews.**

emphasized that in 1745 the concept of 'clan tartans' as deliberate marks of identity was still unknown. Indeed, it was precisely for that reason – because Highland clothing was so successfully established as the Jacobite Army's uniform – that the wearing of kilts and tartans was afterwards proscribed by the government.

A1: Alexander Grant younger of Shewglie

On 12 September 1745 the Laird of Grant's factor in Glen Urquhart complained that 'last night two of Shewglie's sons went off to the Highland armie with a dozen young fellows, amongst which were Alexander Grant in Inchbrin, who wanted to be your forester, and James Grant his brother, who were the only two worth while went with Shewglie's sons; for all the rest was only servants to some of the tenants.' The sons in question were Alexander and Robert; joining with their kinsman, Patrick Grant of Glenmoriston, they served in Glengarry's regiment at Prestonpans and in England. Robert was then killed at Falkirk, but Alexander led the Glen Urquhart men at Culloden. Afterwards he escaped to enter the East India Company service, narrowly avoiding the Black Hole of Calcutta, and fighting at Plassey. This reconstruction, based on contemporary portraits, depicts a typical Highland officer. There are no indications in the hundreds of witness statements that Jacobite officers bore any 'marks of distinction' denoting their status, other than the quality of their clothing and equipment, and perhaps the red tartans seen in many portraits. Note the neat and close fitting way in which the plaid is worn under the jacket and waistcoat; and the fact that the kilt portion is pleated all the way around the front as well as at the rear, and so lacks the flat apron common to modern garments.

A2: Highland clansman

Not many clansmen had the opportunity to choose whether to 'come out' as Shewglie and his friends did. At the other end of the scale was Donald Beaton from Tiree, a petty thief who 'Was with ye rebels 2 or 3 days and knows not the Regt' (it appears to have been MacLean of Drimnin's). Unsurprisingly, he and half-a-dozen other equally uncommitted heroes from the island were simply turned loose.

This altogether less prepossessing figure is based on another Hebridean: a fully clothed early 18th-century murder victim recovered from a peat bog at Arnish Moor on the island of Lewis. Strikingly, he wears a coat but neither plaid nor breeches and is wandering around in his shirt tail. This practice was surprisingly common, and is confirmed both by contemporary descriptions and by an illustration of the 1730s in Edward Burt's *Letters from the North of Scotland*, depicting a man standing in Inverness marketplace wearing just a shirt and coat (see opposite). The most likely explanation is that the plaid or kilt was simply left off as being too bulky and inconvenient if boat work or indeed any other heavy work was in prospect, especially in warm weather – a practice that was still to be seen amongst off-duty Highland troops in World War I. It was also not unknown for plaids to be discarded before going into battle, although the shirt tails might then be tied between the legs. Certainly after Prestonpans, Prince Charles Edward was heard to comment with evident amusement that his Highlanders had lost their plaids. Typically, this man is armed with a French M1717 firelock and has an obsolete French powder flask and ball bag equipment, seen here rather casually carried 'inside out'. Many of the Penicuik sketches seem show Highlanders with bayonets permanently fixed, presumably because they had no other way of carrying them.

A3: Highland clansman wearing plaid

Based on one of Burt's 1730s illustrations, this figure by contrast shows a clansman wearing both belted plaid and trews or *triubhs* in the expectation of bad weather. Since most of the Jacobite campaign was fought out over the winter of 1745/46 in snow, wind and rain, this particular combination of clothing may have been a good deal more common than might otherwise be expected. Note how the tartan for the trews characteristically has a much smaller and simpler check than that used for plaids and other garments, and is also cut 'on the cross' for greater flexibility. This man is armed with a British Long Land Pattern firelock and fixed bayonet.

B: LORD LEWIS GORDON'S REGIMENT
B1: Colonel Francis Farquharson of Monaltrie

Taken prisoner at Culloden, Monaltrie was sentenced to death, but reprieved and pardoned on condition of residing in Hertfordshire, which he did until eventually allowed to return home in 1766.

James Logie recalled that when they marched into Aberdeen in February 1746, Monaltrie's battalion from upper Deeside 'were dressed in Highland clothes mostly', and that Monaltrie himself had a 'white cockade and a broadsword – not in Highland dress'. On the other hand, Allan Stewart saw him wearing a short coat and pair of trews at Inverness; and shortly before the battle of Culloden 'I remember to have seen said Colonel Francis Farquharson with a big blue coat on at the head of his regiment'. Presumably it was a riding coat, like the 'jockey coat' Lieutenant James Stormonth of Lord Ogilvy's Regiment also wore over his Highland clothes.

B2: Major David Tulloch of Dunbennan

Early in the Rising, David Tulloch of Dunbennan, near Huntly, helped raise upwards of 200 men who went into the second battalion of the Duke of Perth's Regiment, while he himself returned home as second-in-command of Avochie's Strathbogie battalion. The most intriguing feature of Dunbennan's outfit in his portrait is the popular black-on-red 'Roy Roy' check used for his jacket and probably, as shown here, for his trews as well. Exactly the same sett with a very dark blue-on-red check is also worn in portraits of Lord Ogilvy and at least one of his officers, raising the possibility that it may have been adopted as a uniform in some Lowland units.

B3: Volunteer, John Gordon of Avochie's Battalion

Orders given to one of Avochie's recruiters on 6 December 1745 stated that: 'All men are to be well cloathed, with short cloathes, plaid, new shoes and three pair of hose and accoutred with shoulder ball gun, pistols and sword.'

Portraits tend to show a certain degree of commonality in the tartan setts used for the various garments, and all of the setts depicted here are old ones. The 'short cloathes' referred to by Gordon – the coat and waistcoat – generally follow contemporary styles, except for being 'bobbed' or shortened. It should be noted, however, that although obviously more convenient for wearing with a plaid, short jackets and waistcoats were also widely worn in Lowland areas. This individual, kitted out in accordance with the instructions, is armed with his own Glasgow-hilted broadsword, and one of the hundreds of French firelocks run through the blockade. Muskets or carbines were pretty much de rigeur for Jacobite leaders, so this man could represent either an ordinary volunteer or a junior officer.

C: LOWLAND INFANTRY
C1: James Moir of Stonywood's Battalion

Like A3, this man, belonging to one of Lord Lewis Gordon's battalions, is dressed for bad weather, wearing a typical suit – in fact two suits, worn one on top of the other – of Lowland clothing recovered from a body found at Quintfall Hill in Sutherland. The various shades of brown almost certainly result from prolonged peat-staining, and the garments may originally have been a much lighter grey.

A nice study by the Penicuik artist of an almost military-looking Highland sentinel wrapped in his plaid; again, see Plate A3. (Author's copy)

On 9 February 1746 Donald Farquharson of Auchriachan wrote to Stonywood offering, 'If you want any Highland plaids or tartans for the men, acquaint me, and I'll endeavour to provide you in some.' In fact it appears from a variety of depositions and confessions that few of Stonywood's men wore Highland dress; a witness named James Logie stated that 'In Aberdeen they dress as I do; a Lowland town.' Instead their likely appearance can be reconstructed from these deserter advertisements appearing in the *Aberdeen Journal* just a few years later:

'John Beverley, born in the parish of Old Aberdeen and lately servant to James Christie, horse-hirer in Aberdeen... had on when he deserted a drab coloured coat with metal buttons' (John Beverley may in fact have been the same man as one of that name who served in Stonywood's battalion during the Rising). 'John Gordon, born in the parish of Belhelvie, a tailor... had on when he deserted a dark blue coat with a velvet neck, scarlet belt, black plush breeches, large silver buckles on his shoes...' 'Alexander McIntosh... an inhabitant of Marnoch (Banffshire)... a labouring servant, had on when he deserted a short grey coat and waistcoat and brownish breeches...' 'William Young, 33, a tinker... wearing a red frieze coat, an old tartan vest and philabeg, and worsted stockings...' 'George Smith, 19, labourer in the parish of Cairney... had on when he deserted a grey coat and tartan waistcoat, grey breeches and stockings...' 'John Archibald, 40, shoemaker... went off in a short brown coat and old green waistcoat, blue breeches with black buttons, and black striped stockings with a broad saddle girth around his middle.'

Typically, this man has a French M1717 firelock and long-branch bayonet, together with a powder flask. There are no indications that cartridge boxes were issued to Jacobite soldiers, so presumably any musket balls or pre-packed cartridges are stuffed in his pockets. In addition he carries a short-bladed hanger; how common these were is uncertain, but James Logie remembered that all of the men at a pay parade in Aberdeen had swords (he also mentions that when they marched out of the burgh 'most of the foot had bayonets'). At any rate William Leith, one of Stonywood's men, mentioned that 'his Arms were taken from him by the Grants as he came South after the Battel [Culloden], except a Hanger, which he delivered up to Mr Chalmers'. As to other equipment, watching them preparing to march out of Aberdeen the Rev John Bisset noted that 'they had on their wallets and pocks, in a posture of marching', and there are frequent references in orderly books to ensuring that canteens were filled.

C2: James Crichton of Auchingoul's Battalion

This figure is based on one of the deserter descriptions quoted above, and also on one of Edward Burt's illustrations from the 1730s depicting a Scottish fisherman being carried out to his boat – a number of those men recruited in Aberdeen by Auchingoul, including John Duncan, John Main and John Mason, were 'white fishers', while William Williamson was a salmon fisher. Note the heavily ribbed

David, Lord Ogilvy (1725–1803). The commander of a two-battalion Lowland regiment raised in Forfarshire, Ogilvy is depicted wearing a red tartan jacket with a plain dark blue 'Rob Roy' check – see also Plate B2. Although there is no evidence to support a suggestion that this particular tartan may have served as a regimental uniform, the frequency with which it turns up in contemporary portraits attests to its popularity, and to its ready availability when large quantities of 'Highland clothes' were required, so the theory is at least plausible. (Private Scottish collection)

knitted stockings (the 'striped' ones mentioned in the description of John Archibald above), which were a staple export from Aberdeen at this period. Auchingoul's corps was hardly one of the Jacobite Army's finest, being both small and poorly disciplined. The kirk session record of Essil, dated 22 February 1746, noted that: 'The rebels of his [Auchingoul's] Regiment were very unruly and showed little regard to his authority.' They also appear to have been badly armed, perhaps because no-one was responsible for them. After their arrest John Duncan and John Mason declared that they were not issued with any arms until they reached Inverness.

C3: John Roy Stuart's Regiment

As usual, the officers belonging to this unit, known as the 'Edinburgh Regiment', normally wore 'Highland clothes', but this soldier wears the 'long clothes' more common in urban areas. He is a composite figure, closely following both one of the Penicuik sketches depicting a Loyalist volunteer recruited in the same area where Stuart picked up so many of his original men, and a set of clothing from an early 18th-century body found at Gunnister in Shetland. His equipment comprises the usual French firelock and this time one of the obsolete powder flask and ball-bag equipments to go with it.

D: DUKE OF PERTH'S REGIMENT
D1: 'Redcoat'
A considerable number of General Cope's men taken prisoner at Prestonpans were persuaded to join the rebel forces, and various Jacobite orderly book entries shortly afterwards refer to the 'redcoats' of both John Roy Stuart's Regiment and the Duke of Perth's. This man is a former member of Lascelles' 58th/47th Foot, still easily identified by his red coat with white facings, although he has discarded his gaiters, and has prudently replaced his hat with a blue bonnet and a white cockade. At least two men from this regiment, Thomas Harvey and William Roberts, were afterwards picked up trying to re-enlist at Stafford. Their story was that they had escaped from Edinburgh, and were only trying to rejoin their unit. Understandably enough, their appearance so far south – when they could more easily have gone to Berwick or Newcastle with other, genuine escapees – aroused suspicions that they had actually been with the rebels, and Harvey at least was subsequently sentenced to death at Carlisle, although later pardoned on condition of enlistment. Nothing more is known of Roberts.

D2: Major James Stewart
One of the Jacobite officers particularly noted as commanding some of those 'redcoats' was Major Stewart of Perth's Regiment. Captured at Culloden after having his horse shot from under him by one of Kingston's troopers, Stewart was found guilty but subsequently pardoned. Like other Jacobite officers he was frequently seen in Highland clothes and armed with the obligatory broadsword. At his trial, Sergeant Allan Stewart of the Appin Regiment testified that just before the battle of Prestonpans the major was one of a party which crept into a coal pit to observe Cope's army. To do so he has replaced his riding boots with a pair of knitted woollen gaiters of a style popular amongst Scottish farmers. At the time, declared the witness, Stewart was also 'dressed in a short coat and plush breeches and wearing a bonnet… observing [his] side breeches pockets to be very bulky, [he] took out a pistol from [his] pocket. He thereupon produced out of his other pockets two small pistols, and two others of a larger size with double barrels… at the same time [he] had a blunderbuss across his arm.' Interestingly enough, another officer of the Duke of Perth's Regiment, Captain James Johnstone, is also known to have been armed with a blunderbuss, as was his sergeant, John Dickson, so carrying them may have been a regimental affectation. The all-brass pistol being shown off here by the heavily armed major is a contemporary Scottish four-barrelled revolver, a precursor of the pepperbox.

Typical fishermen in the 1730s, from Burt's *Letters from the North of Scotland*. Although the naked legs of the women were evidently of greatest interest to the artist, this provides a good impression of the 'Lowland' clothes referred to by James Logie – see Plate C1 and C2.

D3: Manchester Regiment
This unit was originally formed out of a cadre of volunteers belonging to Perth's Regiment. Trial evidence relating to the regiment's officers only refers to the almost universal wearing of tartan sashes or plaids, the inevitable white cockades, and for some of them tartan waistcoats as well, while at least one had a gold-laced hat. Intriguingly, however, a contemporary history of the campaign by Andrew Henderson declares that the rank and file of the regiment were dressed in 'blue cloathes, Hangers, a Plaid sash and white Cockade'. These were presumably some of the same coats worn by the Prince's Lifeguard, hence the red cuffs depicted here.

E: CAVALRY
E1: Lord Pitsligo's Horse
In keeping with their 'Highland' image, most Jacobite cavalry were dressed in Highland clothes of some description. For example, Adam Hay of Lord Pitsligo's Horse was described by one witness as 'dressed in highland dress and armed with a broadsword'; while Andrew Sprule of the same regiment

was 'in his boots, dressed in a highland coat'. Sir William Gordon of Park, on the other hand, sounds as if he may simply have been going through the motions when he was seen wearing 'a sort of highland clothing'. Like most Jacobite cavalrymen this man is armed with a firelock, which may have been in imitation of regular dragoons but more likely reflects his primary role as a scout and skirmisher.

E2: Scotch Hussars

This figure is largely based on two of the Penicuik sketches depicting the hussars – a species of cavalry hitherto unknown in Britain. Exactly why this unit was so designated is not known, but the caps look very similar to recently obsolete French hussar caps, so it is possible that a quantity of them were carried as part of the *Le du Teillay*'s rather miscellaneous cargo. One eyewitness at Carlisle referred to them as 'high rough red caps, like Pioneers'. The best description came from someone in Kendal, who wrote that 'They have several young Men clad in close Plaid Waistcoats, and huge Fur Caps, which they call their Hussars; but they have such scurvy Horses, that I have seen several of them exert all their Vigour to bring them to a Gallop; in Spite of which the poor Beasts immediately fell into a Pace more suitable to their Age and Infirmities.' Another witness, again referring to their tartan waistcoats, also spoke of their wearing 'limber', i.e. supple boots.

E3: Volunteer, Prince's Lifeguard

Equally distinctive were the Lifeguards, and this figure is based on a number of accounts all referring to a handsome coat of 'blue turned with red' and a red waistcoat. The coats were unlaced, but a letter written from Leith shortly after Culloden related that, 'The Pretenders Life Guards have suffered greatly. A person, this moment arrived, saw 26 of them in a heap, with the lace cut off their vests, and their tartan belts lying beside them.' The reference to the belts is confirmed by a description from an English volunteer named James Bradshaw who was 'dressed in long blue clothes turned up with red, and a shoulder belt mounted with tartan.' Presumably these were carbine belts rather than sword belts, since it was the practice in both the British and French services for highly decorated examples to be worn by household troops. The blue coats with red facings were almost certainly French; there is no mention of their being made up while the army was at Edinburgh, and the frequency with which they are mentioned – being worn by the *Companie Maurepas*, the Lifeguards and the Manchester Regiment as well (see D3), indicates that they must have been some of the military supplies carried to Scotland on the *Le du Teillay*.

F: ROYAL ÉCOSSOIS

The ordinary uniform worn by this regiment of Scots mercenaries raised by Lord John Drummond is well documented by French sources, but some interesting variations appeared during the Jacobite campaign.

F1 & 1A: Officer of Grenadiers

This figure is dressed exactly according to regulations, in a dark blue coat lined white with facings of *rouge a l'Écossoise* – red with an orange tinge – and a waistcoat of the same,

17th- and 18th-century Scots bonnets. Although occasional examples are found which have been made by sewing together pieces of woven cloth, by far the greater number are heavily knitted, as shown here.

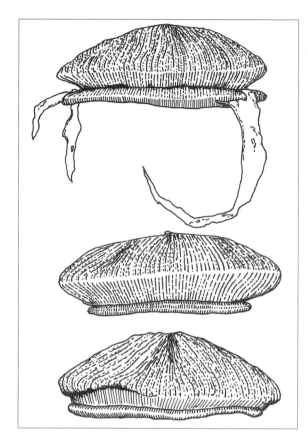

with silver lace. Rather unusually, he wears a British-style mitre cap; the example illustrated, which still survives, originally belonged to one of five officers captured aboard a blockade runner called *L'Esperance* in November 1745.

F2: Piper

The late C.C.P.Lawson asserted that the regiment's grenadiers wore Highland dress, but although no contemporary evidence can be found for this, one man who certainly would have worn it was Lord John Drummond's piper. His precise status within the regiment is uncertain, but – following the example of the well-known series of portraits of members of the Laird of Grant's household – he is depicted here wearing Highland clothing, including the same plaid shown in a contemporary portrait of Drummond himself.

F3: Fusilier

Two descriptions survive of the uniform worn by the regiment while it was serving in Scotland. A drover named John Gray saw Drummond himself wearing a short blue jacket with red facings and silver lace, and a blue velvet bonnet; while a witness at the trial of Lieutenant Charles Oliphant declared that the 'Prisoner wore the uniform of Lord John Drummond's officers, viz: short blue coats, red vests laced [,] with bonnets and white cockades'. Presumably the same Scottish-style cropped coats and blue bonnets were also worn by the rank and file fusiliers, together with the standard French infantry equipment.

G: IRISH PICQUETS
The three regiments illustrated in this plate are the original Irish Picquets, commanded by Lieutenant Colonel Walter Stapleton of the *Régiment Berwick*, which landed in Scotland late in 1745.

G1: Fusilier, *Régiment Dillon*
Apart from their red coats and distinctive colours the Irish regiments had ordinary French infantry uniforms and accoutrements. *Dillon* had black collars and cuffs on the coat, with white linings, waistcoat and breeches, and yellow hat lace. Note the red lace loops linking the two rows of buttons on the waistcoat.

G2: Fusilier, *Régiment Lally*
The newest-raised of the Irish regiments, *Lally* had green collars, cuffs, linings and waistcoats, white breeches and yellow hat lace. The waistcoat is in the same style worn by *Dillon* but lacks the lace loops linking the two rows of buttons.

G3: Officer, *Régiment Rooth*
Captain Thomas MacDermott of this regiment testified that 'Many French officers got highland clothes as a protection against the highlanders who joined us'; while another, Captain John Burke of the *Régiment Clare*, more explicitly declared that 'I wore the highland habit to avoid danger in travelling in red clothes'. This officer has compromised by wearing a plain greatcoat over his scarlet regimentals with dark blue facings and lining and gold lace.

H: OTHER IRISH TROOPS
In addition to the original three picquets, a detachment from the *Régiment Berwick* and a fair number of individuals (chiefly officers) from other units also served in Scotland. The *Régiment Bulkeley* had basically the same uniform as *Lally* but with white hat lace, while *Clare* had yellow cuffs, linings, waistcoat and breeches and white hat lace.

H1: 'Volunteer', Guise's (6th) Foot
A considerable number of former British soldiers were found amongst the prisoners after Culloden. Some were serving in regiments such as the Duke of Perth's, but most had been pressganged into the ranks of the Irish Picquets; it is perhaps little wonder that they fought so desperately. In fact some 60 per cent of the Picquets were former British soldiers, nearly all of whom – like this member of Guise's – were still wearing their old uniforms. Apart from the obligatory white cockade, all that marks him as a member of the Picquets are his French accoutrements and a M1728 firelock.

H2: Fusilier, *Régiment Berwick*
Although this unit shared a colonel proprietor, the Duc de Fitzjames, with *Fitzjames Cavallerie*, the two regiments had quite different facing colours. In this case the 40-odd men commanded in Scotland by Captains Nicholas de la Hoyde and Patrick Clargue had white facings. Note that there are no buttons on the rather plain cuffs.

H3: Trooper, *Fitzjames Cavallerie*
Most of this regiment – better known as Fitzjames's Horse – were captured at sea, but one complete squadron commanded by Captains Thomas Bagot, Patrice Nugent and Robert Shee landed at Aberdeen in February 1746. They brought ashore so much of 'their horse furniture, arms, breastplates and baggage' that they required nine or ten carts and 20 pack horses to carry it all. About 70 men were mounted at Culloden, while the remainder presumably served on foot with the rest of the Irish Picquets. Whether the mounted men actually wore their breastplates at Culloden is unknown, but as their horses were in poor condition it seems unlikely that they would have burdened them with the extra weight.

Another of Maclan's paintings, giving a good idea of just how voluminous the belted plaid could be.

INDEX

Figures in **bold** refer to illustrations.

64th Highland Regiment (British Army) 12, **15**

ammunition 49–50
Appin Regiment, colours **25**
armaments 46–50
arms (heraldic) *see* colours, banners and flags
artillery 41–3
Athole, LtGen the Duke of 44
Athole Brigade 6, 7, 8, 13, 15–16, 54

baggage train 43
Balmerino, Arthur Elphinstone, Lord **14**, 28
Bannerman of Elsick, Sir Alexander
   Regiment of 16, 20
      colours **17**
banners *see* colours, banners and flags
bayonets 47, 48, **48, 57**
Berwick Regiment 30, 32
Black Watch Regiment **9, 15**, 48, **58**
Blair Castle 43
Bland, humphrey 53
bonnets **62**
Bowey, Robert 12
British Army
   64th Highland Regiment 12, **15**
   1727 *Regulations* 53
   deserters 12–13
   recruitment from defeated Jacobites 57, 61
Burnet, Capt John 41

Cameron Clan
   and recruitment 6–7
Cameron of Locheil, Donald 5, 45
   Regiment of 15, 16
      colours **17, 18**
Carlisle 46
cavalry units 14, **26**, 26–9
Chisholm of Strathglass, Roderick Og
   Regiment of 17
      colours **18**
Clare Regiment 30
clothing **61**
   see also uniforms
colours, banners and flags **16, 17, 18, 19, 20, 22, 23, 24, 25, 30**
command structure 43–6
conscripted forces 10–11
Cope, Gen Sir John 5, 12, 41
Crawford, John 9
Crighton of Auchingoul, James
   Regiment of 17
Cromartie, George Mackenzie, Earl of 58
   Regiment of 7, 8, 15, 18
Culloden, battle of 3, 45, 47, 48, 51, 52, 54, 55, 56

Daniel, John 28
Dawson, Jemmy 9–10
d'Argenson, Marquis 29
d'Eguilles, Marquis 31, 32, 41
drill training 50–5
Drummond, Lord John 30
Drummond of Melfort, LtCol Lord Lewis 41
Duke of Perth's Regiment 5
Dutch forces 30

Elcho, Lord 28
equipment **51**
Erroll, Lady 8, 20
Etat Major (French ship) 45

Falkirk, battle of 30, 31, 41, 42, 43, 45, 52
Farquharson of Monaltrie, Francis
   Battalion of ('Mar' Battalion) 18
feudal allegiances, vassalage and levies 7–8, 10, 15
firearms *see* guns
Fitzjames Cavallerie **26**, 27, 28, 30, 31
flags *see* colours, banners and flags
Fontainebleu, Treaty of 29, 30
Fontenoy, battle of 41, 42
Fort Augustus 43
Fort William 43
French forces 13, 29–30, 31, **31**, 32, **32**, 41, 56

Gardes Francais **31**
Glascoe, Lt Nicholas 30, 46, 54
Glengarry, Lord
   Regiment of 15
Gordon, Lord Lewis 10

Regiment of 14, 18, 19
Gordon of Avochie, John 6
   Battalion of 19
Gordon of Glenbuchat, John 6, **11**, 46
   Regiment of 19, 48
      colours 19
Gordon of Park, LtCol Sir William **29**
Grant, Col James 41
Grant of Glenmoriston
   Battalion of 19
guns 47, 48, **48**, 49

Hamilton of Sandstoun, John 9
Hawley, LtGen Henry 43
Hazard, HMS 43
Highland Regiments 5
Highland Visitors (Dubois) **6**
Highlanders and soldiers **7, 12, 57**

Incident in the Rebellion (Morier) 54
infantry 15–26
Irish Brigade (French Army) 13, 30
Irish Picquets (French Army) 30, **31**, 31–2, 56

Jacobite uprising origins 3–4
Johnstone, James 46, 50, 53–4

Kilmarnock, William Boyd, Lord 8, **13**
   Horse Grenadiers of 27, 28
   Regiment of 17, 19–20, 55

Le du Teillay (French ship) 41, 46
Le Renommee (French ship) 42
L'Elisabeth (French ship) 32
L'Esperance (French ship) 32
Lifeguards 28
Lion, HMS 32
Lochaber Axes 47, **49, 50**
Locheil *see* Cameron of Locheil, Donald
Louis XV, King of France 29
Lovat, Simon Fraser, Lord **10**, 57
   Regiment of 14, 20
      colours **20**
Low Country Foot 5
Lowland units 5–6, 10, 15
Loyalists volunteers 12

McBean, Rev Alexander 13
McBean, Maj Gillies **55**
MacDonald, Col Sir John 30
MacDonald Clan
   and recruitment 7
MacDonald of Barisdale, Col
   Regiment led by 14
MacDonald of Clanranald
   Regiment of 21
MacDonald of Glencoe
   Regiment of 21
MacDonald of Kepproch
   Regiment of 21–2
McDonnell, Col Sir John 45–6
MacDonnell of Barisdale
   Regiment of 20–1
MacDonnell of Glengarry
   Regiment of 14, 21
MacGregor Clan 22
McGrowther, Alexander 8
McIan, Robert
   paintings of **4, 7, 12, 26, 42, 44, 55, 63**
MacKinnon of MacKinnon
   Regiment of 22
Mackintosh, Lady
   Regiment of 22
MacLachan Clan 22
Maclaren, Capt John 8
Maclaren, Peter 8
MacLean Clan 22
Macleod, John Mackenzie, Lord 18
MacPherson, Cluny 12
   Regiment of 23
Malt Tax 8–9
Manchester Regiment 23
Maurepas Company 32
mercenary forces 10–11
Moir of Stoneywood, James 9, 10
   Battalion of 24
Murray, LtGen Lord George 16, 43, **43, 44,** 45, 52, 53, 55
Murray of Broughton, John 26–7

Nairne, Lord 16

O'Bryen, Col 29
Ogilvy, Lord David 11, 48, 53, **60**
   Regiment of 14, 15, 24, 48, 50
      colours **23, 24**
organization of Army 13–15
O'Sullivan, Col John William *see* Sullivan, Col John William

Penicuik sketches **3, 8, 12, 21, 27, 28,** 47, 48, **49, 52, 53, 56, 59**
Perth, James Drummond, LtGen the Duke of 8, 44, 45
   Regiment of 13, 24–5, 41
Perth, John Drummond, Lord 45
Pitsligo, Lord
   Horse of 28
plaid, kilts and tartan **4, 7, 9, 12, 26, 42, 45, 53,** 58, **58, 59, 60, 63**
pressed forces 5–8, 10
Prestonpans, battle of 3, 5, 12, 41, 51, 52
prisoners of war 56–7

recruitment 6–13
   composition of army 3
   mercenary forces 10–11
   motivations for joining 8–10
   pressed forces 5–8, 10
   rent based 10
Regiment d'Albany
   colours 20
Rooth Regiment 30
Royal Ecossois 30, 32, 41, 55, 56, 57
   colours **30**
Ruthven Barracks 43

Scotch Hussars 26–7, **27**
Shetland ponies **26**
shields 48
Stewart, Ensign 49, 50
Stewart, John 8
Stewarts of Appin 25
Strathallan, Lord
   Horse of 27, 28–9
Strathboggy Battalion 10, 19
Strathbogie Regiment 11
Stuart, Charles Edward, Prince (Bonnie Prince Charlie, The Young Pretender) (1720–88) 3, **4, 5**
   arms of **20**
Stuart, John Roy 54
   Regiment of 26
Sullivan, Col John William 14, 30, 32, 43, 45–6, 50, 52
swords 46, 47, **47,** 48
swordsmen **3, 8**

tactics 50–5
Townley, Francis 23

uniforms 58
   Fusilier, Regiment Berwick **H2**(40), 63
   James Crichton of Auchingoul's Battalion **C2**(35), 60
   Col Francis Farquharson of Monaltrie **B1**(34), 59
   Trooper, Fitzjames Cavalerie **H3**(40), 63
   volunteer, John Gordon of Avoche's Battalion **B3**(34), 59
   Alexander Grant younger of Shewglie **A1**(33), 58
   volunteer, Guise's 6th Foot **H1**(40), 63
   Highland clansmen **A2**(33), **A3**(33), 59
   Fusilier, Irish Picquets Regiment Dillon **G1**(39), 63
   Fusilier, Irish Picquets Regiment Lally **G2**(39), 63
   Officer, Irish Picquets Regiment Rooth **G3**(39), 63
   Manchester Regiment **D3**(36), 61
   James Moir of Stonywood's Battalion **C1**(35), 59–60
   redcoat, Duke of Perth's Regiment **D1**(36), 61
   Lord Pitsligo's Horse **E1**(37), 61–2
   volunteer, Prince's Lifeguard **E3**(37), 62
   Piper, Royal Ecossoirs **F2**(38), 62
   Fusilier, Royal Ecossois **F3**(38), 62–3
   Officer of Grenadiers, Royal Ecossois **F1**(38), 62
   Scotch Hussars **E2**(37), 62
   Major James Stewart **D2**(36), 61
   soldier, John Roy Stuart's Regiment **C3**(35), 60–1
   Maj David Tulloch of Dunbennan **B2**(34), 59

volunteer forces 8–10
   Loyalists **12**

Waverley (Scott) 3
weapons 46–50
Wentworth, Maj Hu 16
William, Duke 8